Transformed

MARY JANE

ISBN-10: 0615732208
ISBN-13: 9780615732206

Transformed website:
Transformed-woman.com

Mary Jane & Transformed
P.O. Box 6792
West Palm Beach, FL 33405

This book was designed and proofread by
Alchemy Communications Group
A Regan Communications Company

Creative Director: Steve Owens
Editorial Director: Kelly Owens
Videographer: Scott Zimmer
Editorial work: Winifred Storms
                          Dan Ewald

Original Creative Designer: Mary Mayhew, Big Shoe Creative

FOREWORD

BY SIMON T. BAILEY

Author of *Vuja de Moment*

Years ago, I met a woman who possesses "the peace that passes all understanding." Believe me, if you saw her, you'd know it, too. There's just something about her mien, though she's not particularly beautiful or elegant, that causes one to look twice and to wonder what secrets she holds. She'll tell you that even the plumber who came to her house one day to fix a leaky faucet commented on it; the mailman, too. The truth is that woman's palpable inner peace didn't come naturally or easily. When she was in her twenties, she was raped and left for dead. She had to fight for her life, overcome hurt and shame, and ultimately forgive her tormentor to achieve something few of us call ours, that thing, that peace, that unites us with the rest of the world and owes everything it is to God himself.

Today, I introduce you to another woman, Mary Jane, who knows that peace, too. She also had to fight for it, overcome much and forgive. This is her story you are about to read. Her battle, like many people's battles, was against low self-esteem and high self-absorption, quick fixes and long unremembered episodes, anger and hurt, drugs and more drugs. What makes it, I think, more relevant, more compelling and, yes, better than other stories of its ilk is its simple and resounding underlying message: to be truly free you've got to rely on God, to be content with life you've got to let go of earthly expectations and let God be your guide, to be a responsible adult you've got to be accountable to Him, and to love fully you must first love yourself as a child of God.

Maybe some people don't need a wake-up call to live freely and fully. Maybe some can find true peace without tragedy and trouble. Maybe some can live in holiness and wholeness without God. But maybe, too, that's because those who have gone through the deep dark tunnels, those who have fallen into the abysses, and those who have known hopelessness and helplessness have bared their souls, shared their stories, and shown the way.

I think that in the biggest way possible we're all searching for peace. We fight with each other, we fight with ourselves, but in the end aren't we all really fighting just to be heard? So maybe the peace that passes understanding, when it all boils down to it, is being truly understood and loved, flaws and all, for the people we are and the voices and values we have.

If that's the case, read on. Be thankful for what Mary Jane has gone through, perhaps for your benefit, and allow yourself to be forever changed.

Intimate thoughts from those who lived with me, watched me and loved me while I suffered, very nearly died and recovered:

"When the experts said to let her go, I refused to give up. Driving the streets all hours of the night, hoping to find her so I could bring her home, was hell for me--- knowing this was like finding the proverbial needle in the haystack. I was not going to let go. I did pray a lot and God answered my prayers." — Dad

"Having witnessed addiction in a loved one and losing my son… M.J.'s story gives unvarnished insight into addiction…Helping us understand there is a way out if there is faith! The greatest gift we give our children is the love of God. As parents this story may help you understand that we need to have strength and fight for all we are worth… know the true meaning of tough love!" — Karen H.

"An enlightening recount of a young woman's fight to take back her life. Her story is a winding journey through countless struggles and numerous memories, both good and bad. The courage, strength, and security she found through faith to overcome and never give up on herself proves that people can change. 'Inspiring,' 'graceful,' 'motivating,' 'brave,' 'kind,' 'best friend,' and 'beautiful' are words I use to describe the woman I know and love with all my heart." — Lynne

"I watched my friend, incapable of grasping the rigorous honesty that it took to save her own life, spiral into the pit of hell, which I thought she would never come out. M.J.'s recovery is a true miracle." —K.K.

ACKNOWLEDGMENTS

To my much-loved and faithful family, best friend, soul-mates, and mentors--- Thank you for inspiring me to stand in the abundance of God and tell my story of redemption.

To the addict or alcoholic who still suffers in darkness---This story of overcoming the shame and power of addiction is dedicated to *you*. I encourage you to walk towards the light of God and experience the truth, freedom and restoration recovery promises.

PROLOGUE

The once richly decorated hotel room was demolished: the bed ripped from its frame, the wallpaper scraped down to the bare wall, the tasteful pictures torn from their hooks and turned backward so the cameras couldn't see me, and the air conditioning unit destroyed beyond repair so I could get at the roach-like spies I was convinced were nesting in the unit's grid.

I couldn't remember how I'd gotten here, barely functioning after ten days awake and hiding out, scarcely eating and sleeping, not knowing how my skeletal, 100-pound body found the energy to cause such damage.

Though the past days had come and gone with no record of dates or times, with one fading into another, I knew that the damage I caused this time was more than physical. It was more than spiritual. It was a battle to the death with God and me on one side, and the Devil and his minions on the other. But in my life journey, the Devil went by a different name, and his name was "the Great Destroyer."

I took a big hit out of a long glass pipe filled with last night's residue. The intense rush exploded in my head and I instantly became more paranoid and skittish. I hid the remaining drugs and my paraphernalia under the seat cushion, tucked away behind the zipper so no one could find them. The morning light intruded through the curtains, taunting me with the possibility that today might be the day that I could muster enough courage to go home where my loving husband and daughter waited for me.

As quickly as I had hidden the drugs, I was digging my pipe out again. Another hit brought flashing memories like an online digital slide show, reminding me of a few places I went during this run that I'd rather forget: inside dangerous drug dealers' homes, shady liquor stores, and endless filthy rooms of crack addicts who shared my hunger to get high over and over again. Yet, spending time around lowlife drug addicts still made me anxious and frightened.

And yes, I was acutely aware of the irony and arrogance behind that thought.

To look at me then, you would have sadly dismissed me as just another low-class, uneducated crackhead. But I wasn't. I had it all — beauty, education, financial success, and, most importantly, love. But that was before I threw it all away for crack. My face was drawn, with hollow cheeks and sunken eye sockets. My chin had small red sores from stress, constant picking, and lack of nutrition. I tried desperately to hide the scars on my face by wearing heavy foundation, full make-up, and lip gloss. My bloodshot eyes were swollen from crying. The dark circles under my eyes told the story of a scared, lost woman rushing headlong toward death and destruction. My disheveled hair was tightly pulled away from my face, and my pathetic, tiny body was covered in wrinkled, dirty clothes scented with cigarettes, cheap perfume, and booze. I disgusted myself.

I had been hiding out for a week and a half trying to decide when I would start communicating with my exasperated husband, Chris . We were still newlyweds and I was wracked with guilt. Such a gentle soul didn't deserve to marry someone with the heartbreaking issues I had hidden from him. He was still hurting from what happened during our recent wedding ceremony.

I picked up the receiver to call him, but it seemed unusually weighty. Were phones always so heavy? I knew I had stayed in this place far too long. With barely any sleep, I felt death's presence oppressing me. This was an upscale hotel – $150 a night – and too many days of denying the maids admission to clean made me feel as if I was under suspicion. Management must know something was going on. It was only a matter of time before they pounded on the door for answers.

I finally called Chris and told him for the first time in ten days I was ready to come home. He agreed to rescue me but didn't sound relieved. Anxiously, I packed my suitcase with filthy clothes. I wanted to clean the room, ashamed of the destruction I was leaving for the hotel staff. I couldn't lift the artwork back onto the walls, so I just left them leaning against the floor. There was no way I could put the air conditioner back together … or repair the gouged wallpaper… And forget about the condition of the bathroom. Where would they begin?

Paranoid beyond belief, I craned my neck out the door, making sure the halls were clear. I needed to bolt from the room so the housekeepers wouldn't see. God knows what they were going to find in there. Had I stuffed all the drug paraphernalia in my bag or was some of it still under the sofa cushions?

Instead of taking the elevator, I sprinted toward the staircase where there would be less human activity. Bounding down several flights, the luggage hit both walls with reckless abandon, dragged behind this frail, sick-looking young woman. At the bottom of the stairwell, I parked my suitcase and perched upon it, waiting for Chris to arrive.

I thought the back door would be safer. Instead, it turned out to be the staff entrance, and the morning shift was arriving. Shiny, well-adjusted people streamed through in their starched uniforms with rehearsed smiles on their faces. Technically, for the next few minutes at least, I was still a guest of the hotel, so I suppose they had to pretend not to notice what a hot mess I was. I had bloody sores on my chin from nerves. I had picked the scabs more than once and my face was looking rough. Although my broken demeanor cried out for compassion, I knew they looked at me with disgust and wondered what on Earth was wrong with me.

Thirty long minutes dragged past and Chris still hadn't come to rescue me, so I called him again. He reassured me he was on the way.

I took a deep breath to relieve some of the anxiety, thinking to myself, *"In a few minutes I will be out of danger. I won't have to look over my shoulder anymore or wonder if the police are looking for me. When the drugs wear off, I can take a shower and wipe off the sweat and filth. I will try to eat before I fall into a deep sleep. My body will once again begin to heal itself from ten long days of abuse."*

Chris's black truck pulled into the lot and I was ashamed for my new husband to see me like this, the once-beautiful, polished bride he fell in love with now a broken and unkempt addict. Through the windshield, I watched his face change from disbelief to sadness. His heart must have been tearing as he saw me leaning against my suitcase for support. I stumbled over to the truck and tried to lift the bag.

Chris got out and threw it in the backseat. "I have conditions," he said, buckling me in like a helpless baby. Our eyes connected, which felt embarrassing and beautiful at the same time. "You can either go to treatment or you can go back upstairs to hell." He told me he had changed the locks on our house and I was no longer welcome. He had packed clean clothes for me, which explained the other piece of luggage in the backseat.

I was furious as we pulled onto the highway ramp. I was <u>not</u> going to treatment! I tried to explain that all I needed was to go home and sleep it off. I knew I could do it on my own. I promised him it would never happen again.

His cell phone rang. Chris answered it and told the person on the other end that I was not willing to get help.

"Who are you talking to?" I barked.

"Susan is a woman who is willing to help you get addiction treatment," he said, pointedly. "She wants to speak to you." I was appalled he thought I needed help but took the phone, nevertheless. This Susan woman tried to coax me into treatment, saying I needed to accept my condition. She didn't know who I was. She didn't know I was smart and educated enough to see through her manipulative "sales pitch." I had kicked this drug thing before – on my own terms – and I would do it again now.

AUTHOR'S NOTE

In order to get clarity during the blackouts and gaping holes of my life, I've included commentary from my family and a few close friends for this book. They will frequently weigh in and share their perspectives because I want you, the reader, to understand the consequences of my choices on those who loved me and were there every step of the way.

Addiction impacts the lives of so many people, not just the addict, so it's only fair to have them share their stories. I didn't take this journey from hell by myself, and couldn't have made it home without them.

CHAPTER ONE

I had every advantage a person can be given in life: a loving family, wealth, education, and beauty. No one could understand why a girl with my background would willingly throw away her late twenties and early thirties – the prime years of her life.

When I was a little, my dad worked for Allstate Insurance and moved us from Chicago to St. Petersburg, Florida. All four of us – my father Joe, mother Leigh, my little brother Chad, and I – quickly fell in love with the state of sunshine, palm trees, orange groves, and beaches.

Unlike my Illinoisan family, landlocked away from ocean tides, swimming pools and sunshine, I was a water bug and had a natural talent for swimming. There was a drive within to excel at the sport, and I performed my swim laps with dedication and focus as far back as first grade. Afternoon practices ended with us kids walking home exhausted, eyes bloodshot from the chlorine, wrapped in towels, leaving a trail of water drops on the sidewalk the Florida sun and wind quickly evaporated.

Every athlete needs a good nemesis, and my competition was a girl named Dawn. It always came down to the two f of us when they were handing out the blue ribbons. My stroke was the butterfly and my dad spent endless hours at the pool helping me to improve. If I came in second to Dawn, I was mad and inconsolable for days at a time. It wasn't in my nature to come in second.

This dedication to be the best was contested by my second-grade teacher, Mrs. Miller, who became fed up with my stubborn unwillingness to follow directions. One day she called my mom and asked, "What is wrong with Mary Jane? She just will not listen in class. Does the child ever do anything without discussion?"

"No, she does not," was the reply.

Eventually my teacher figured out the problem and called our house again.

"I think Mary Jane acts out because she can't hear me."

Her diagnosis sent me off to auditory testing sites. Seated in a cold glass bubble, I remember the ear doctor slipping a big pair of Seventies earphones on my little blonde head. BEEP, BEEP, BEEP went the sounds in the headset. I raised my right or left hand, indicating in which ear I was hearing the noises. I tried my best to answer correctly, but, sadly, this was one contest in which I wouldn't take first place. The audiologist concluded I had a hearing impairment of such severity that I was categorized as legally deaf.

Trying to discover whether or not I had severe allergies that would affect my hearing and my ability to communicate with the world, they gave me a series of shots underneath the skin along my back to see what normally harmless substances could be causing my hearing challenges. Sometimes I went to medical offices two or three times a week, sometimes every day. I got so tired of entering those automated hospital doors that slid open and shut. One day I refused to walk through them and hid in the bushes out front.

The gig was up when the looming figure of a heavyset woman appeared in front of me, backlit, like the cover of Stephen King novel. She was the intimidating nurse who had pricked me with a needle many, many times to deliver a dose of medicine that prevented my ears from clogging up with fluid. The sting of the medication entering my arm was a daily reminder that I wasn't like other kids. At one point, I went every day after school to maintain a balance between my hearing and the buildup of liquids that would fill my ear canal while shutting me off from hearing my family, teachers, and friends.

"Mary Jane!" she bellowed. "Don't make me come into those bushes and get you! You come in here and get these shots."

I had dozens of surgeries in a short period of time. The doctors put tubes in my ears to open up the canals. Nothing really came of all this time on the operating table, and my hearing never really improved. Being partially deaf left me out of conversations at school. I was a chameleon of sorts, often unable to comprehend what people were saying but trying to guess and adapt. I naturally thought kids were always talking about me when they would look my way and laugh. My discomfort likely drove me to become the competitive swimmer I was; I didn't need to hear underwater to fit in with the crowd. I was on an even playing field when in the pool. Having to put Vaseline and lamb's wool in my ears and a tight rubber swim cap over my head made me stand out, but being different pushed me to greater successes from this point forward: in sports, school work, and later, my choice in careers.

My mom recalled…

It was very difficult for Mary Jane. I did not realize it at the time. In second grade she came home from Catholic school and said, 'Mom, what do you think your cross is?' I asked her what she meant. She said, 'Everyone has a cross to bear and I know what mine is. It's my loss of hearing.' She knew that and really struggled with it. As her mother, my heart broke to hear my seven-year-old talk about this heavy burden. She knew then she was different from her friends.

At swim practice, the team clique made me feel like an outsider. We were all competing for first place, so I'm sure that had something to do with it. I loved to win swimming ribbons and medals because I felt accomplished, as if my hearing loss, the funny looking Vaseline and lamb's wool, time away from school and hospital visits didn't matter. No, in those moments, I was a strong and healthy instead of a sick little girl who generally felt out of place. But even at birthday parties the girls were mean to me, teasing me about my hearing impairment until I cried. I was the odd man out in that environment. Yet, I couldn't figure out why; I believe that I was simply an easy target in the world of "girls being girls."

Eventually, I became so self-conscious about having to use lamb's wool and Vaseline, and so lacking in self-esteem due to my hearing loss, that I decided I didn't want to swim anymore because I thought I looked like a boy. Despite my long, curly blonde hair and my flare for stylish, feminine clothes, my back was muscular, defined, and strong. It was taking on the shape of a "V" and didn't feel feminine to me. My dad thought I was nuts. "How could *you* look like a boy, Mary Jane?" he asked in disbelief.

But I knew I needed to stay involved in sports in order to fit in and remain in touch with my friends. Plus, I loved athletics; the art of competition, the thrill of winning, and the sting of defeat. It motivated me, as it does even today.

I was also a cheerleader from first grade through college. Being on the squad meant the world to me. I remember my friends and me spending the day at the Wet 'n' Wild water park, trying to distract ourselves from the fact that we were waiting to find out who would be cheering that year.

When I discovered I hadn't made it, I "went hysterical," according to my mom.

Her life was over, she was so angry! There was no losing with Mary Jane. She wanted to find a way to change the captain's picks, but what could she do to change it? She was like this throughout the whole growing-up period – competitive and on a mission to find a place to fit in.

CHAPTER TWO

My competitive nature probably kept me alive in my ten-year fight against drugs – that and the grace of the Lord. For a decade, I was prey to the demons that roamed the Earth, and I was defenseless against temptation. Others may have the capacity to walk away from the lure of drugs. Because I lacked spiritual wisdom and discipline, I couldn't. Despite the discouraging pattern of four failed rehab treatments and multiple relapses that marked those years, I always held onto the hope and sense of connection I found in God ever since I was a child. The fact that a drug addict can even have a relationship with God might surprise some, but I loved God even in the darkest hour of my active addiction.

This desperate letter, written during the height of my drug addiction, illustrates God's presence in my life during that time.

～

Dear Mom and Dad,

I can't seem to quit writing. I only wish I could talk to you again, to tell you how sick I really am right now. Yet the phone in the hotel won't call long distance.

For some (and I pray I'm not one of them) the addiction envelops every cell. It saturates your body with enough craving and chemicals that it is almost impossible to stop. I'd say that in a way, I've become "brainwashed" by what I've seen, heard, felt, and done while high. It transforms me into another person – a woman I do not know or like. The woman that is sitting here writing this is afraid of living because, in my opinion, my life is a failure and has lacked any real success in the last five years.

I don't tell the truth most of the time. I just drift from conversation to conversation, switching the truth to fit the person in front of me. There is a voice within me that wants to scream, "Help me, I am dying!" yet there's another voice telling me that I can still "pull this off" – I can quit if I just try one more day.

I spoke to you, Mom, last night and you were overwhelmed with questions and fear. Dad, you didn't even say hello to me. I know my disease, my addiction, is a heavy burden to those who love me and are close to me. My chronic habit will kill me, and destroy the faith of some and sadden the hearts of those who believe in Christ. Yet they are the ones who better understand the spiritual warfare that takes place within the souls who have Christ, yet have seen, felt, and experienced the lure of the enemy's tactics to destroy.

I have upset my family again! It never fails. I will do whatever it takes to get and stay well. I've lived a double life. This time I am going to internalize my journey and take every step to become the woman of love, dignity, and grace that Jesus created me to be. I am committed to growth and truth.

I will keep my eyes focused on who I was before I tried crack. I will not believe the lie that I am not worthy or capable of maintaining and enjoying a sober life, serving others. I have come to a place that I would never have believed possible in my life. I am a prisoner again of crack. It's noon and a breezy, beautiful day yet I sit in a crappy hotel needing sleep, food, and help.

I want to be free, yet I am held captive in my own skin. My spirit, the spirit of my inner child, has been beaten up so many times; I think I've almost given up. I am fearful that I cannot recover. My friend Artie told me just two days ago that the odds are against me. Very few crack addicts recover.

I am fearful as I fall asleep, wondering who will break in and hurt me while my eyes are closed. Intense anxiety is part of how I live and function. I have been afraid my entire life. I don't know how else to live. I've forgotten what it feels like to be in a strong, beautiful body. I am now weak, thin, and my face looks drawn and broken out.

Oh how I miss you, Mom and Dad. I miss going to church and knowing Jesus is standing next to me. I am going to lie down now ... more later...

MJ

~

My cry to God and to my family wasn't always so drastic and painful. I have had so many wonderful days. As a little girl, I went to church every Sunday and attended Catholic school through middle school. I learned about Jesus from the nuns. Most of the nuns were very nice. They were soft spoken, polite, and told stories about how much God loved us. They shared the stories that Jesus grew up and performed miracles inspired by God. Sister Teresa would tell stories of how Jesus walked on water, healed the sick, made a blind man see, and how He feed thousands of people with only a few fish and a few loaves of bread. My perception of God was that he did a lot for us, and that he loved kids. However, I also had a feeling that bad things happen to those people who sinned, or behaved badly. There were times I was afraid of what might happen to me because I knew I wasn't perfect — and that I was a sinner according to the examples they taught in school.

In second grade, I was in the play *Jesus Christ Superstar*, filling the role of a leper in the background of the scene. Wearing tattered clothes and entering from the back of the darkened church, I loved being part of a show about Jesus, even if He was being played by a teenager with pimply skin.

Of course, the role I wish I had gotten was occupied by another blonde. She played the role of Mary Magdalene. I had such admiration for her acting ability. Those of us playing lepers were on the outside and could only grasp at the Savior's legs. She was front and center in the spotlight, singing a song with her beautiful voice, holding His hand. She was gripped with pain during this scene because she loved Jesus so much and He was going to be crucified. The music, the theatrics, and the other characters brought this moment to life two thousand years later in a small Catholic church. She sang the song, "Jesus Christ Superstar" in such a remarkable way. For me, it was like being on Broadway in New York City. She stood, arms stretched toward the audience, capturing their hearts. Her voice was amazingly wonderful. She sounded like an angel as she bellowed the words toward God. The music was so strong you could feel it in your chest, and it conveyed the message that Jesus was real and that He was the answer.

I always had a heart for Him. The musical at school only made me love Him more deeply. He was just the most beautiful person I had ever seen. I carried a picture of Christ in my pocket, the same picture my Grandma had at her house. In it, He had light skin, a beard, and long hair – nothing like he looked in actuality, I'm sure, but that was my Anglo-Saxon childhood visual. I remember seeing His face on church walls over the years and thinking to myself how fortunate I was to know God's Son.

My family worshipped in typical Catholic fashion. We attended Mass every week and celebrated holidays like Christmas and Easter. For Christmas, Mom always went overboard to make sure it was a wonderful day. My brother and I would come out from our bedrooms Christmas morning and the entire floor would be covered in beautifully wrapped gifts. We tore into the toys and spent the day laughing and playing with everything we received. My parents constantly provided joy-filled holidays. Easter was especially filled with happiness because we had up to 50 neighborhood friends in to celebrate this holiday. We would all play games like "Egg Toss" and "Easter Egg Hunt." Themed years included wearing homemade Easter bonnets, creating a song with Easter-related lyrics, or creating themed T-shirts. It became a tradition everyone looked forward to.

Tirelessly working behind the scenes of all our family holiday gatherings was my mom. She always made an extraordinary effort to create theme parties that would remain in our memories forever.

During my childhood, I couldn't have asked for a more loving and nurturing family, but I still sought solace in Jesus. As a little child, I remember one night hearing a voice. I couldn't interpret what it was saying but I truly believe it was a voice from God that I could barely understand; like a muttering. Sometimes it was louder, sometimes quieter. And then it would go away. The language wasn't familiar to me and at times I was frightened by it because I didn't understand what was being said. One night, alone in the dark, concerned that I didn't understand, I asked God not to speak to me in this way. The murmuring never returned.

Also as a little kid, I used to pray that Jesus would come and sit on my bed, so we could talk about how He could help me fix my hearing problem. I was tired of feeling different, of not understanding what the teachers and my friends were saying to me, and of having to take baths and not showers so my ears wouldn't get wet. *Jesus can help me with that*, I hoped.

CHAPTER THREE

My dialogue with Jesus continued uninterrupted until I experienced the opposite side of the spiritual spectrum when I turned fourteen.

To celebrate my birthday, I invited seven girlfriends over for a slumber party. A sun-filled day at the beach turned into more splashing in the pool at our house. Mom and Dad made burgers on the grill, we shared birthday cake, and I unwrapped gifts from my friends.

Evening rolled in and I decided it was time to kick it up a notch. I walked into the room with my arms full of board games. "What do you want to play?" I asked.

"What's an Ouija board?" inquired one girl.

I hadn't even opened that one. It was still shrink-wrapped, a leftover present from last December. We moved everything out of the way and made a comfortable place next to the bed. The box's instructions told us to light candles and sit in a circle. We were directed to ask questions to the board and it would either answer by moving the pointer to the words "Yes" or "No," or spell out more complicated answers. Several people were supposed to hold onto the pointer, but it supposedly was navigated by spirits beyond this Earthly realm.

For a group of eight teenage girls, it seemed like the perfect game for a slumber party: exciting and a little spooky. We knew it was an interactive game but didn't understand the dangers that came with it.

Quite a few of us touched the pointer with our fingertips and started asking the board questions. At the time, I had a secret crush on Tim Taylor, a cute football player with dark hair.

"Does Mary Jane like Tim Taylor?" my friend asked. The pointer went over to "Yes." Everyone laughed, surprised at its accuracy. One girl accused me of manipulating the board so it would go where I wanted it to go. She asked, "Is Mary Jane moving the Ouija arrow?" and it went to "No."

"Is someone else moving the board?"

"Yes."

"Who's moving the board?"

This is when the so-called game turned creepy. There was trepidation and nervousness among my circle of friends as we stared at one another in the dimly lit room. The arrow moved to the letter "D". And then slowly to the letter "E". I felt my palms getting sweaty. I tried to tell myself that it was ridiculous. Someone else was doing it.

The arrow moved to the letter "V." At that point, everyone else started getting scared. We had secured the board on some books and our knees were touching each other. I could feel the other girls starting to shake. As the arrow shifted to the letter "I," the intensity in the room elevated again.

As the arrow landed on the letter "L," my friends jumped up and sprinted from the room. They were screaming, as though a burglar had just smashed through the window threatening to harm us all. I was the last out and was blocked by our Doberman Pinscher standing in the doorframe. He was barking like a dog consumed with intense fear.

"Sable, it's me! It's me!" I yelled. She seemed to be reacting to the Ouija board and wouldn't let me pass. I was terrified down to my core. The hairs on my arms stood on end and I was covered in goose bumps. It felt like there was someone or something evil in my room that wasn't there moments earlier. Whether there was truly something evil in my room that night, or it was the insanity of teenage girls screaming and running down the hallway in a flash mob, or something darker and more sinister at work, I'll never know.

My mom remembers the evening well.

I can still see Mary Jane in the living room that night. The expression on her face was like one of those movies where a person tries to get the Devil out of his body. She was terrified beyond terrified. I didn't realize at the time how bad it was or how it would impact her later. It was just one of those scary things that kids do when they're sitting around and talking about scary things. Looking back on it now, it's really like an evil spirit attached itself to her that night. That night forward, for several years to come, Mary Jane was petrified to fall asleep and kept the lights on.

I had always felt like there was something out there — a spiritual force battling against God and against us — and now I was convinced of it.

I was always prone to nightmares but the Ouija board scare intensified my dream life. I started to dream about a lady who lived alone in a big, dark mansion. Night after night, I walked inside her creepy home and interacted with her in my nightmares. The Neoclassical house had an enormous rounded entry porch with columns and symmetrical windows along the front. The overgrown landscape, threaded with vines and weeds, made it difficult to walk toward the front door, yet I was drawn to move closer. As I made my way into the residence, dust and phantom perfume filled my nose, and the dry air made it difficult to breathe. The broken furniture was covered in sheets and cobwebs covered the windows. Chandeliers with broken strings of crystals flickered as I walked the down the hallway towards the gloomy staircase. My fingers clutched the banister as I walk up the stairs. Startled, I covered my mouth to stop a scream when I heard the faint sound of a woman crying for help. Chills ran down my spine; I felt death approaching me from every side. I ran toward the closed door, turned the knob, and slowly opened the creaking door. She lay on the floor next to a bed. Each haunted dream was the same - she wore a long Victorian dress, and she would die in my arms crying for me to help her. Her wavy, gray hair was always fastened in a bun, and she looked at me gasping for breath as hot tears ran down my face. I struggled to slow my heartbeat. Then, as she died, I would look down toward her face and she would transform into an older bearded man with gray features, dressed in dark clothes with a raspy voice. In every nightmare, he would threaten me, "If you don't give me your soul, I'm going to go get Allie's. Or Anna's. Or Amy's," he threatened, ready to take the souls of my friends.

The recurring nightmare lasted for four years, until I went to college. This nightmare only intensified my fear of the dark and of going to sleep. Too often, my mom would wake up to see the light on in my bedroom at 2:00 a.m., finding me writing poems and stories, doing anything to keep myself awake, and away from that demonic presence haunting my dreams.

But then, with the introduction of drugs, my nightmares crossed over into my waking hours. I wasn't much a drug user in high school, but in my senior year when I started dating a guy named Ken, we occasionally smoked pot together. One night, when my parents were gone, we lit up a joint and smoked it. Within minutes, I felt like a demonic spirit had entered the house. The hair on my arms stood straight on end, and I became chilled to the bone. I was afraid to turn around, certain I would see the demonic spirit walking towards me. This was the first time I experienced this force outside of my dreams, and it terrified me. The aura in the house shifted, and I felt like an immoral energy force was surrounding me on every side. It transpired in slow motion. I could feel the man from my dreams coming toward me in the hallway.

Even though I couldn't physically see him, I could sense his presence flowing toward me. Tears filled my eyes as I said to Ken, "He's here."

"Who's here?" said my boyfriend, as he laughed, dismissing my fear.

"The man from my dreams is in this house right now," I answered, wringing my hands. He must have thought I was crazy. I had never told Ken about the series of nightmares, which is why what happened next really did me in.

A few seconds after my bold declaration, Ken turned toward me, stared for a moment, and said, "I told you I'd come for you." Flabbergasted, I froze, not knowing what would happen next. Ken and I were separated by a kitchen counter and a small breakfast bar, which gave me some space. I pondered running for the front door to escape the fear and my spiritual monster.

"You are not welcome here!" I shouted. I walked toward the hallway where I knew it was standing, instead of walking toward Ken. "In the name of Jesus, get out!" I could hear Ken laughing behind at me at first, but he stopped when he realized I was serious. As I turned back to Ken, he looked like himself again and not the man from my nightmares. The phantom spirit left the house -- and so did Ken. I didn't want to be around him. I needed time to pray and ask God for forgiveness. I had placed myself in danger by smoking pot. I knew chemicals were referred to in the Bible as partaking in witchcraft. Petrified, that night I slept with the light on, in my brother's room in his extra twin bed.

Of course it's possible Ken was just being an obnoxious 17-year-old boy playing a joke on me. It's possible my hallucination was enhanced by the weed we smoked. But I still believe, years later, that there was something in that moment that terrified me, some wicked energy inside the house that night. What I was too young to understand was I had opened a Pandora's Box that would haunt me and influence my behavior for years.

Even as an older teen, I slept outside my parents' bedroom door so I could be as close to them as possible. I would sleep at the foot of their king-sized bed with my blanket and pillow, or I would crash on the overstuffed couch in the living room just outside their room. Being closer to my overprotective parents gave me some relief. They knew the dreams were very real to me. However, being in close proximity to their door changed nothing about what happened once I closed my eyes. The woman continued to die in my arms and the man kept coming up through her as a demonic spirit. Once the spirit tried to make a bargain for my soul, I would awaken. I was always fearful of going back to sleep because the dream usually picked up where it left off.

The last nightmare happened during my freshman year of college when the demonic being turned his focus on my family. It said one night, "If you don't give me your soul, I'm going to take your dad." At that point, my father entered the dream, and he and I fought the demon before the altar of a church. I remember my dad proclaiming in a loud voice, "This is it! You don't get my soul, and my daughter is not giving you hers!" My dad stood, as the spiritual leader in my life, defending me at the altar inside the house of God. For the first time, the demon retreated and seemed to relinquish its demand for power over me.

I woke in the middle of the night and called my house. I wanted to speak to my dad immediately. I was in one of those emotional states where I was having a difficult time differentiating between reality and my subconscious. My mom told me my dad was in Atlanta on a business trip. I pushed her to give me his phone number at the hotel. I had to be sure he was all right.

I called my father. Of course he was just fine, other than being awakened at that hour. I told him the dream was finally over. And after five-and-a-half years of the ongoing spiritual nightmare, it truly was over. Forever. It never occurred again.

Though the recurring visions of the demonic man left me that night, I did not realize that the demons I would encounter later in life would come in all shapes, sizes, and containers, from pills, to powders, to liquids, to solids. I didn't realize how many disguises the Devil could take until I was introduced to nightclubs, late-night parties, and trance music. Once again, I would open up the closed Pandora's Box.

The Bible says, "Our enemy, the Devil, prowls around like a roaring lion looking for someone to devour" (1 Pet. 5:8). I believe Satan's evil spirits usually infiltrate people through their minds, and Scripture is replete with instructions about properly managing our minds by controlling our thoughts.

By using drugs, I put myself at risk knowing that they created a gaping window into the unknown. Drugs initiated chaos in my soul and produced confusion, fear, and ultimately, contact with demons.

CHAPTER FOUR

My first exposure to drugs was a total mishap. In eighth grade, my friend Julie approached me in the school bathroom. In her hands she held some diet pills she called "Black Beauties." They were "hot" and a teacher was on her trail. She tried unloading the pills on everyone in her path. I asked her what the pills were supposed to do.

"Nothing, just take them. They're like headache medicine."

I suggested she flush them down the toilet but she said she didn't want to waste them.

We had just moved from St. Pete, where I spent all those years sheltered in Catholic school, to Orlando where I was now trying to navigate the big scary world of public education. I just wanted to blend in. Staring at the pills, which I later learned were called "speed," I was a little worried about what I was putting in my body. But the overwhelming desire to be cool took over. I was pretty easily moved, swayed, and bamboozled.

"You'll feel more awake," Julie promised. "We have swim practice later and it'll help us."

It didn't.

I couldn't swim that afternoon. My heart was beating faster than normal and I began cramping. Coach Clay had to hop in the pool and get me because I couldn't make it to the end. Obviously I didn't tell him what I had taken and I never breathed a word about it to my parents. The experience was so unpleasant I had no interest in speed. It certainly wasn't the doorway into what would eventually be my drug habit.

It was the early Eighties and drugs were just starting to enter the public discussion. Nancy Reagan was beginning the "Just Say No" campaign. At school, we were forced to watch a film featuring hippies doing acid. My friends and I laughed, watching the visuals of long-haired, greasy, unwashed relics from the Sixties tripping out on hallucinogens. Bugs climbed all over the camera lens trying to teach us what dropping acid looked like. A bad narrator warned us of the side effects. The film meant nothing to us, other than an opportunity to stop doing class work and laugh at hippies.

This wasn't the stuff being discussed in my home. My parents weren't ones for talking about challenging subjects like sex or drugs. I'm not blaming them, but I was totally unprepared for life outside of our home. I lived in a completely sheltered environment where dangerous subject matter was left unspoken.

I recall sitting at a stoplight in my mom's brown Mercedes, waiting for the light to turn green. I don't know what personal information I was trying to discuss with her but the response made it clear that my conversation was hitting a nerve. "Mary Jane, we don't talk about this stuff outside the family. This is *our* stuff and our stuff only."

While there is obviously such a thing as a "private matter," the message I received from her was, "You shouldn't talk about difficult things. Ever." My mom grew up with a father who drank a lot, and maybe shutting down was her way of coping with that pain.

My father was completely foreign to the world of drugs. He weighs in:

We never did drugs. I wouldn't know what a marijuana cigarette tastes like and that's a pretty good thing. To my knowledge, my wife Leigh had never tried drugs either.

We tried to restrict what Mary Jane could watch on TV, but we knew that when she went to her friends' houses they didn't have the same restrictions that we did. We wanted her home at ten p.m. Her friends didn't have to be home until midnight or later. Their parents could care less when they came home.

Late in her senior year in high school, she began to sneak out behind our backs. She would get home by curfew, say "goodnight" and head to bed at the same time we would. But come to find out, she knew how to turn off the house alarm, sneak out the window, jump the fence, go off with her friends, and come home who knows when.

Our friend Randy walked his dog at one or two a.m. and caught Mary Jane pushing her car down the street to avoid engine noise. She was always doing more than we thought she was ready for.

My dad's memory is correct. I was starting to rebel and my boyfriend Ken only made it easier. He constantly pressured me to sneak out and I didn't want to. I would hang up the phone and he'd call back, over and over again, until I would finally agree to leave my house in the middle of the night to meet him and his friends. My dress code was changing, my attitude turned away from doing the right thing. My brother Chad remembers the tension within the house at the time:

It's the standard mother/daughter thing. Mary Jane was dating a guy and it was an unhealthy relationship, which affected our house because she and Mom were always fighting. Mom is very strong-willed. Our nickname for her is the Ragin' Cajun. When she got mad her eyes kind of bugged out. She was the strict one. She set the rules and always had an opinion.

My mom had every right to be upset with the way I was behaving. It didn't help that she and my dad didn't see eye-to-eye on how to reach me.

My mom explains her side:

Joe and I never agreed on the children. I knew she was on drugs later in her senior year of high school and I wanted her tested. She had changed dramatically. The horrible anger she had between her and me...

One Friday night she didn't come home, so I tracked down her whereabouts and told her to get back to the house. I told Joe to tell her not to leave once she got home. I was working in real estate and had a closing that night.

When I arrived at the house that night, Mary Jane's car wasn't there. Joe was cooking steaks on the grill. I asked him where she was and he said she had gone back out.

I went ballistic!

I had to walk away. I walked for miles. It just didn't make sense to me but Joe and I were never on the same page. I had to ask myself if I thought Joe was stable. Was this really where I wanted to be? How could he not get involved? How could he let her leave again that night?

We had been married eighteen years but we were just miserable during her senior year in high school. I had to decide if I was going to even stay in the marriage. I needed a helper. I had to come to acceptance that Joe was never going to change. He just wanted to let it be, and if you don't talk about it, it doesn't exist.

We finally got Mary Jane to a psychologist in her late twenties because the anger was so horrible; we were worried she could maybe hurt herself. The doctor called us after three or four sessions and said, 'You've got a beautiful daughter here and know that she loves both of you very much. Because of that, she will come through this. Because of her relationship with God, she will come through.' It made us feel good; it gave us hope.

CHAPTER FIVE

Ken and I were on our way to a party with another couple; boys in the front, girls in the back. When he apparently felt the time was right, Ken let us know he had some cocaine in the glove box.

"What the heck is cocaine?" I asked, naively. My boyfriend pulled out a little bag of white powder.

"It's just something you sniff. It wakes you up and gives you energy," he replied. I remember thinking, *we're teenagers – why do we need help in the energy department?*

But he was my boyfriend and I figured, *well, it must be something* seniors *do*. Right there in the car, we all did a small amount of cocaine. I didn't enjoy snorting something through my nose; it felt weird and a little trashy. But the drug only gave me a jolt, and wasn't something I enjoyed all that much

Later that night I arrived home at 10:00 or 11:00 p.m. and caught Dad playing my Journey record on his brand new sound system. "Don't stop believin'" he sang, sitting at the table, sharing beers, smoking cigars, and playing cards with his buddies. I laughed and laughed. He was having a great time with his friends. He and Mom never drank in excess, and I was never much of a drinker, either. Alcohol did a number on my stomach and I didn't enjoy the taste of it. It also gave me terrible headaches. No, drinking never really appealed to me.

The first time I ever tried booze was at Light Up Orlando, a big outdoor party where they blocked off the streets and had DJs spinning music. Ken and I drank Jack Daniels and I hated it. But that's what everybody was doing. I figured if I did it long enough I'd react like they did enjoying the taste, and my body would eventually adjust to the liquor and I could drink like they did.

The party continued at my friend's house later that evening. We played quarters on a table with Jack Daniels and a bottle of tequila. If you didn't bounce the quarter into the cup, you had to take a shot.

On the way home, I was so sick in Ken's Bronco truck. I was in the backseat clutching my stomach, rolling around, wishing I never tried a sip of Mr. Daniels. When I got home, there was no hiding from my parents that I was wasted.

The next morning, I wanted to call in sick at my job in the Snack Shack at the tennis club. I had my first hangover, and the worst headache of my life, but my dad wasn't having it. He made me go in. After an hour or two on the job, my hangover still persisted so I called home to ask if I could leave early. Dad's response was, "If you want to drink with the big dogs, you got to go to work with the big dogs."

At the same time I was learning how to manage a part-time job, I had the added responsibility of supervising my younger brother. Chad was a freshman during my senior year, and he loved the fact that he never had to take the bus to school. I was his ride; I was also his ticket to all the upper-classman parties. Being a good-looking, blond charmer, Chad was always popular at school. The night the Homecoming Queen was to be crowned during halftime, Chad got the whole freshman football team to rally around and vote for me. I was his hero.

I cheered for the first part of the game, and at halftime went back with the other girls to change from our uniforms into our homecoming dresses. I wore a baby blue strapless dress with white ruffles that complimented my long, blonde curls.

Those of us nominated were driven back out onto the field to the fantastic roar of the crowd. We sat atop a convertible and waved at the fans in the stands. I felt popular and beautiful, and it was quite a rush.

Each girl was announced with tidbits of information about her hobbies and interests. I stood between Julie (my speed "pusher" in eighth grade) and Sally, and held my breath in anticipation. Last year's Homecoming Queen, a redhead named Michelle, held the crown in her hands.

I squinted to see my supportive family in the stands. Mom and Dad were cheering. Chad and his teammates were in their freshman football uniforms, chanting my name.

Michelle opened the envelope and paused. The longest pause, ever. In that moment my mood went from excitement to fear. I thought, *if I win, these girls are going to hate me.* My insecurities were forgotten the next moment when Michelle read my name: "Mary Jane. Mary Jane Smith!"

I won. I was crowned Homecoming Queen. The next hour of my life was an exhilarating time of congratulations and celebratory hugs. I was doted upon by everyone except my selfish boyfriend Ken, who wasn't about the share the spotlight. Standing off to the side in his tight jeans and Black Sabbath T-shirt, Ken looked agitated and impatient with the whole scene.

So, he left me on the field and just took off. Getting a lift to the after-party wasn't the issue; it was being ditched by my narcissistic boyfriend on such a momentous night for me.

A few days later he and I hadn't really made up. I threatened to go to the Homecoming Dance with another boy, which changed Ken's mind about not going. He agreed to take me but wasn't thrilled about it.

Ken and some of our friends did cocaine before heading to the hotel. I did not. Ken then combined coke with drinking, getting completely wasted before we even arrived. He was so high he couldn't get out of the car. I hadn't had any alcohol other than a champagne toast my parents gave us on the way out the door. I was sober.

I walked up to the Disney Hyatt, solo. Everyone had dates on their arms but not me – not the Homecoming Queen. The idiot I called my boyfriend was so plastered he couldn't make it into the hotel. Sitting alone at the table, I waited for a half hour. People kept stopping by, asking me where my boyfriend was. Eventually, I had enough and charged back out to the parking lot in a fury.

Ken was doubled over next to a tree, still trashed. I barked, "If you don't get your butt up right now and sit down for dinner – this is it!"

He stumbled in a few minutes later and joined me at the table. I made him dance with me a couple of times.

You might think after that evening that Ken and I would have been finished for good, but we dated off-and-on into my freshman year of college. Now, looking back at how I got so far off track, I realize that I lacked both a connection to God and any feelings of self-worth. Even then, I was empty and searching for something outside of me to fill the void deep within my soul.

My mom weighs in:

Mary Jane and Ken finally broke up their freshman year in college, and our sweet daughter returned. She allowed him to upset her. She surrendered her peace of mind and her morals dating him. It was terrible to watch Mary Jane sacrifice her all-American-girl virtues for a head-banger who treated her so poorly. She never dated anyone like him again.

CHAPTER SIX

Some people hate college; some love it. For me, college was the time of my life. I attended the University of Central Florida while Ken went to Florida State University. We were four hours apart. My parents paid for my education and made it very clear that I would not be attending the same school as my boyfriend. I originally wanted to follow Ken to FSU and study physical therapy. My parents' reaction was, "Over our dead bodies! We are paying for your education. You're not going anywhere that guy is." Ken was blamed for the late-night parties, the downbeat change in my behavior and attitude, the sneaking out of my house, and the overall approach to my last semester in high school. I was overwhelmed with trying to win his affection, so making a healthy choice to step away from him wasn't easy. Instead of standing up for myself and knowing I was worth being treated with respect, I simply caved and was treated like a doormat.

I begged and pleaded, but my parents were clear it wasn't up for discussion. They didn't even want me visiting Ken. Of course, I saw him a few times behind their backs, but our relationship ended when I discovered he had begun dating one of my best friends from high school. I felt betrayed at the time but, in retrospect, it was for the best. My former best friend Melissa was also a head-banger who loved heavy metal, like Ken's favorite bands Black Sabbath and Iron Maiden. They were practically twins in their skintight jeans, smoking cigarettes and wearing their favorite rock band T-shirts. I *did* fantasize about slashing the oversized tires on his black Ford Bronco while they were upstairs in their shared FSU apartment. I also wished for the day I'd run into her socially so I could ask, "What kind of friend goes behind someone's back and starts dating her boyfriend? A slut? A liar? A thief?" I would have used that conversation to purge all my frustration and pain, so it is better we never again spoke. Ken always made me feel bad about myself, commenting that I was "fat" or that I didn't look good in my size-two jeans, which was ridiculous. I was a champion swimmer, a cheerleader, and worked out all the time. I was voted Homecoming Queen! But Ken was domineering, overprotective, and macho, so he controlled me by belittling me. I was a pushover, I guess.

I swore to myself I'd never date a guy like that again. My college boyfriends after Ken were smart, successful, and treated me like a lady. For two-and-a-half years at college I dated Bobby, a super-cute, marvelous, nerdy engineer – but a cool nerd, the total opposite of the handsome and dangerous Ken. Mom and dad liked Bobby, though they knew he was just a college crush.

Bobby and I had so much fun together, dancing at the clubs or sharing great meals poolside with other college couples. We spent hours together studying in the library, and many nights cheering for our much-loved sports teams at our favorite college hotspots. Bobby and I had a wholesome and healthy relationship, but we were just too young to see how good we had it.

I did well in school, maintaining a "B" average. At first I was a Liberal Arts major, but then turned my focus to Communications and Marketing. I joined a sorority, Zeta Tau Alpha, and had many female friends inside that sorority house. It was perfect, just like a movie scene about how college should be — from all-night study sessions downstairs cramming for exams to pillow fights to break the late-night doldrums, interrupted by inspirational chats about who we hoped to become after graduation. Being in the sorority was never-ending social scene. The frat guys would bombard our house, running through the hallways, picking us up over their shoulders. We also were always invited to the most elite frat parties, like the themed Lambda Chi Hurricane Party or the Alpha Tau Omega Viking Social. We also had wonderful teaching moments through doing service for Zeta; we had the chance to work with children, or create activities on campus for the other students. The lessons the sorority taught during Sunday house meetings included etiquette, career coaching, and essential life skills. As part of the student government group, I met men and women alike who also had a heart for making UCF attractive to future students. We worked long hours planning the incoming freshman retreats, when each of us took a group of ten to 20 students under her wing for the entire week. It taught me to genuinely care for others and their future at UCF.

When I wasn't with Bobby, my sorority sisters, or the student government, I was cheerleading. We practiced diligently five days a week in preparation for the game on day six. I loved everything about being a UCF cheerleader, from the pep rallies to the performances.

There was nothing more intoxicating than being at a football game with 15,000 people watching us cheer. As the "fly girl," I was thrown four stories high, amazing the crowds with back flips or full twists. I would do back-handsprings across the football field behind two fantastic tumblers, Lisa and Brandy. I loved to make the crowds cheer "U-C-F." A perk of being a cheerleader for a Division I football team was traveling and meeting really cool people everywhere we went. It was such a perfect time in my life: I had a boyfriend who loved me (and who my parents liked), I was doing well in school, and I had a rich and positive social life that didn't involve drugs or alcohol. Even my relationship with God became stronger; I thought God had answered my prayers. I finally felt that I belonged.

During winter break my junior year, I invited all my friends to my parents' massive holiday party. I figured, the more, the merrier.

I mentioned it to my parents, who prepared for a few more guests, but I didn't realize just how many of my friends would actually show up. I should have known better; I'd left a message on the answering machine in my dorm room three weeks beforehand saying, "If you're calling about the Christmas party, here's the date and location of my parents' house." Close to a hundred people lined the block to attend that night. Fortunately, we lived on a golf course with plenty of space to overflow. That Christmas party was a huge blowout and a night to remember. Mom and dad played traditional Christmas songs, served warm holiday food, and made a fire out back for everyone to enjoy. The holiday party was about God, and college friends, and family. I believe we made an impact in the name of God's glory on our guests that night, simply through the act of hospitality.

The huge Christmas party reassured me that I was no longer an outsider. Finally, I was accepted and admired. Sure, there was always a girl more popular than me, but I had no real reason to complain about anything in my life.

Yet I was still drawn to the outsider, the guy or girl in the back of the room who didn't have friends. I wanted the outsiders to know that I understood. I knew how they felt. Losing some of my hearing at a young age had left me on the outside, looking in, so I empathized with feeling left out.

One night, Bobby and I visited my friend Amy at University of Florida. Over the course of the evening, she started going on and on about this pill called Ecstasy. She'd been doing it for years and wanted us to join in on the fun. I was really resistant. I had avoided drugs since high school and felt no need to start that craziness again. I had been totally drug free with very little alcohol intake for four years.

She told me to try a half a pill. There we were, in her boyfriend's fraternity house, going back and forth about this stupid little pill. Ultimately, I caved and popped it in my mouth.

I leaned back into the couch and waited to feel the effect of the drug. It didn't take long. Staring up at the ceiling fan, I thought, *"That is so cool. It just goes around and around and around."* I felt free. I had never felt so relaxed and comfortable in my skin. I felt beautiful and more confident. I felt what I imagined to be "at peace." Honestly, it was a great night. I had never experienced someone else's skin feeling so comfortable next to mine. Holding Bobby's hand was really incredible. My senses became so heightened and my ability to express my thoughts and emotions became so effortless that I wanted to feel that way more often. I sat with Amy for hours, talking about life and honestly sharing about my secret hopes and dreams in a way I had never expressed before.

After that night, Ecstasy became my constant companion. It was a fun, social drug, a way for me to go out with people and stay up late. My friends drank a lot, so I took half a pill of Ecstasy to feel part of the group.

Now in my final two semesters in college, and with cheerleading practices over, the drug started to fill the void in my schedule. It made me feel beautiful. Even though I was already a social person, "E" made me feel even more so. I didn't look into the dangers of the drug. I just remember my friend John telling me that Ecstasy used to be legal in his home state of Alabama, claiming he used to pay a $10 cover charge to get into a bar where he got a drink coupon and a hit of Ecstasy.

I thought, *well, if they're giving it away at bars in Alabama, there must not be anything wrong with it.*

Ecstasy became popular with all of my girlfriends and college buddies. Looking back, it really became an epidemic. Thousands of seemingly smart, high-performing college students became part of this weekend subculture.

We got dressed up, had dinner, took some Ecstasy, and went dancing inside warehouses where late-night raves were all the rage. Girls were dressed in psychedelic outfits, sucking on pacifiers, wearing their hair in pigtails. At the other extreme, there were beautiful young women dressed like movie stars, smiling and enjoying the club's atmosphere. There were guys hallucinating in the corners of the room while dancing wildly to loud music. It was a spectacle encompassing all walks of life, including mine. Though I considered myself normal compared to those I described – I was still involved in this subculture, dancing center stage, high on Ecstasy, and loving the entire experience. The music came from gigantic speakers and bounced off the walls. I could feel the bass in my chest. The extensive laser light shows in hues of red, blue, and magenta created waves of emotions among the crowd; the community would cheer, in awe of what the DJ and light technician could create. Circus acts such as tightrope artists and acrobats in body paint occupied the air space above the crowd to keep the audience engaged. Exotic and strange performers danced, using trancelike gestures inside cages and behind silhouette screens. Intoxicated, everyone appeared to have the freedom to dance, laugh, and be their true selves. We *did* stare at the strangest of the rave-goers, yet they really didn't care what anyone thought of their hair, what they wore, their rhythm or lack thereof, and from that perspective they were appealing. As the sun rose, everyone went back to their respective homes. The next day, we got up and carried on with our lives. Most of the time, our meager hangovers and few other repercussions allowed us to live like those who went to bed at a decent hour. Yet I knew, from watching the severest outsiders and the most extreme spectators inside those warehouses, that some didn't fare quite so well.

CHAPTER SEVEN

Though my college life was amazing, as the saying goes, all good things must come to an end. Bobby and I broke up before senior year. I was progressing towards graduation from UCF, but during my last semester I went out dancing with my girlfriend Lauren one night. We headed to a trendy club called JJ Whispers where there was an attractive police officer named Mitch working security at the door. With his handsome face, big blue eyes, and sexy uniform that fit like a glove, I was hooked.

After few weeks of flirting with Officer Mitch, I gave him my phone number. Once we started dating, I decided there was no point in trying to hide my drug use from him, even if he was a cop.

Because his assignment was stopping gangs and not narcotics, he had a lax attitude towards my recreational drug use. Though he said he couldn't do it himself, he'd look the other way if I decided to partake occasionally in Ecstasy.

Mitch and I had a ball together. We went on vacations. We loved the beach. We loved family gatherings. We went dancing with friends, cheered on our football team during tailgate parties, and had season tickets for our favorite professional basketball team, the Orlando Magic. Mitch and I never fought — we were a great couple.

During the final semester of my senior year in college, I came home and told my mom I had a job, but there was a chance she might not be happy with it.

"You're not working at Hooters, are you?" she joked, which was hilarious because yes, that's exactly where I had found employment. Our Hooters restaurant was more of a wholesome "All-American" place, I told her. It wasn't full of slutty vixen waitresses in Day-Glo orange hot pants. We were just normal girls working our way through school. The day I graduated from college in the spring of 1992, I was promoted from waitress/bartender to marketing manager for two stores.

While working at Hooters, I befriended a girl named Allison. She introduced me to her closest friends: Nine gorgeous girls who often competed in the Hawaiian Tropic pageants and fitness challenges. The best thing was they were as nice as they were beautiful.

We worked together at Hooters. We were hot young women who were truly living the dream: Residing in the chicest areas, making lots of money, driving expensive cars, buying designer clothes, and getting into the most exclusive clubs. We worked and played hard. But our collective group took a sharp left turn when we re-discovered cocaine. When we would go out, I was enjoying two tablets of Ecstasy without any negative consequences, so I felt ready to put cocaine back in the mix. Our routine each weekend quickly changed. We did Ecstasy to get ourselves charged up on the dance floor, and once we danced the night away, we would head back to someone's house and break out the cocaine. That kept us awake from Friday after work through mid-morning Saturday, when we would finally go to bed, sleep it off, get up and get dressed, go out again, and keep the party going through Sunday.

However, my cop boyfriend was getting in the way of my partying. When he proposed to me, I told him I needed some time to think it over. The social conflict was compounded because he didn't fit in to my late-night excursions. He didn't like raves or large nightclubs. He didn't love trance or house music, and some of my so-called friends didn't want to have a cop as part of our scene. Mitch didn't want to have dinner or social conversations with any of my circle. After some time, and emotional confusion, I said "yes" to his proposal. That just thrilled my parents; they loved Mitch and were delighted I had found someone so kind, responsible, and hard-working.

Unfortunately, I eventually started to feel differently about his job. It was becoming more dangerous and paid horribly, so I broke off the engagement. I was young and terrified I would lose him to gang violence, plus I had the impression that police officers live meager financial lives. My family thought I was ridiculous. "Are you nuts?" they asked me, with good reason. "This guy is a great family man, incredibly loyal, a hard worker…"

I knew all of this and loved Mitch, but I wasn't ready to get married. He was five years older than I and ready for the next step. I had different ideas about what the future would hold, yet I had no clue what was actually in store as my life took a turn, hell bound into an abyss of destruction.

Adding coke was the beginning of my search for a better high, for that perfect pharmaceutical combination. At some point, my nine best girlfriends and I worked in another drug called "itchy-scratchy," a liquid that was sniffed. To this day, I have no idea what it was made of. We also experimented with another liquid drug, GHB, but that was something we drank by the capful. It made your feet feel as if they had twenty-five-pound weights attached. When on GHB, it became hard to walk so I would have to sit on the stairs leading up to my second-floor apartment because I couldn't make the flight of stairs in one try. Driving was impossible.

The high was never enough. We eventually tried adding acid to the mix, but I found this hallucinogen to be a horrible. The video with the hippies we mocked back in high school was oddly accurate. When tripping out on acid, a nearby TV or a lamp could come alive, as if I could see the individual molecules vibrate inside an inanimate object. I only did acid a few times because it was just too freaky.

The consequences of my drug use started to catch up with me. While my girlfriends laughed and joked around while high, I became silent, introverted, and reclusive. Maybe my chemical makeup was different, because when I started mixing cocaine with Ecstasy, my body and my mind said, "I can't handle this." I began feeling left out again, just like when I was a child with a hearing impairment. I was once more the outsider and believed the group didn't like me anymore. Soon, paranoia became my frequent and unwelcome companion.

One night, I tiptoed over the sleeping bodies crashed out on the couches, floors, or any flat surface they found. I grabbed the wall for balance and managed to stumble into a bathroom. I stared at my sad reflection in the mirror over the sink. My hair was pulled back in a tight bun, which was a sign of my life descending into misery. It was 7:00 on a Sunday morning and I was miserable. That was the first moment I realized that I didn't party like my friends. They had a higher tolerance for drugs. They could socialize and laugh and look like they were enjoying it. I was really struggling. Outside the bathroom door was a room full of my girlfriends, sleeping off the night before, resting to prepare for the week ahead. Not me. I was alone in my misery.

Stepping back into the hall, I ran into my friend Dave who had been downstairs partying with the guys. "Are you okay?" he asked. I was humiliated because I felt that he knew my secret. He saw something different about the way I was handling the drugs and constant partying. When I didn't answer, Dave grew deeply concerned and asked, "Mary Jane, are you okay? Do you need to lie down?" I said nothing and quickly left the house as though I was OK. I sped out of the driveway in my brand new Montego Blue Mazda RX7, fleeing from my closest friends. I remember how scared I was being outside on such a beautiful morning. The contrast between God's glorious sunlight and my dark secret was confusing, furthering the chaos in my mind and emotions.

Allison confronted me a few days later. "Mary Jane, what's wrong with you? You always disappear from the party. Where do you go? You don't tell anybody; you just leave."

She was right. The partying that had been a Friday-to-Saturday event had become a Thursday-through-Monday morning thing. Recovery time had narrowed down to Monday through Wednesday, and I wasn't handling it well. The nights partying were becoming longer and more intense. To cope, I would turn antisocial.

I quit laughing and having fun with my friends. I stopped going out on the dance floor. I went from a social Ecstasy user to a hardcore drug user. I went from enjoying social activities to wanting to disappear. I remember walking into a T.G.I. Friday's for dinner with my girlfriends. Because I worked at a popular Top 40 radio station, I was still incredibly popular and would get stopped along the way to my table. At one point, I remember thinking *I just wish I could get from the door to the table without anyone knowing me.* Being popular and trendy taxed my deteriorating state of being. I was embarrassed, and my inner struggle and outer appearance began to look the same. Acquaintances began asking if I was sick. I was leading a double life. My conscience was constantly reminding me of the gap between my portrayal and my reality.

CHAPTER EIGHT

After breaking off my engagement to Mitch, I decided that living with four of my party friends was a fantastic idea.

Prior to my big job at the Top 40 radio station, I worked at Dekko's Night Club, an Orlando hotspot open seven nights a week. It was my job to book the entertainment, write the radio commercials, and design billboards to promote the business. Unlike so many other graduates, I really was putting my marketing degree to good use.

My boss, Michael, owned the club but worked as a criminal defense lawyer during the day. He taught me a lot about running a business, and was incredibly particular about details. I became a valuable member of the team, but my drug use wasn't escaping notice. One day Michael pulled me aside and said, "Look, I can't really put my finger on all of it, but I know something's going on. Let me buy you one visit with this lady." He handed me the card of a therapist named Sally. Michael may have had no way of knowing that, even at work, I always carried a bag of cocaine in my pocket, but he was smart enough to be aware something was very wrong. He said I needed to seek help if I was going to keep my job.

I went to see Sally, and was appalled and insulted the first time she labeled me a drug addict. I had seen drug addicts on the street and was nothing like those sad losers. An alcoholic or drug addict was dirty, homeless, and lived under a bridge while I was a pretty blonde, a college-educated woman with an impressive job. Yet Sally was relentless, not letting me hide behind my façade. She taught me to look for similarities to other addicts, to look for ways I resembled other people suffering from the same illness. Sally was the first person who ever told me that I would die from addiction if I didn't get help. She shared a common phrase used among those in recovery that I found to be truthful -- addiction inevitably leads to "jails, institutions, and death." We spent more time together in the months that followed. Sally would remind me, "Anything you place before your recovery you will lose." Sadly, I did not realize how prophetic Sally's warning was.

One night while I was high and hanging out at a dingy pool hall, I saw myself in a stranger. I memorized his body language, and his voice echoed in my ears as I compared his outside behaviors to how I felt about myself inside. Later that night, I wrote about it in my journal:

So many feelings right now. I just left a pool hall where I found a fiftyish man so drunk he was talking to himself, aloud. His voice sounded like Sylvester Stallone's. He had thick glasses and a fake leg. I kept wondering how he got to where he is right now. Why does he drink so much? I found myself feeling sad and sorry for him. I guess I also saw some of me in this stranger, hiding from myself while dying to find peace at the same time. Ironic, isn't it? You know that not using can set you free, but you continue to sabotage your life anyway.

Lord, this is a request with admiration and respect... Save me from myself. I know You can literally "save me." I try to love all people for who they are. I've made mistakes and plenty of them, but I do not want to be a sinner, Lord. I want to be a servant of Your Word. I want to be a messenger.

If you can hear me and my request to better my life, to find peace, and leave all substances, I will promise to be a prophet to spread Your love to everyone I come in contact with. I am your servant. I am your child. I ask with gratitude for all you've done already. Lift this cross of mine. Help me to say, "No!"

I have no need for these substances. I need Your mercy and strength. I beg You to walk with me and give me courage. I believe and I want to show others. Amen.

I think the first time my parents had a clue about my problem was when my mom stepped through the front door of my condo one afternoon without an invitation and I didn't welcome her. I did not greet her as a normal, healthy daughter would. We had family in town visiting from Chicago. While my relatives chatted with each other downstairs in my living room, I was up in my bedroom, uptight, fidgety, fearful, and gakked out of my mind.

My mom and my cousin said, "Come downstairs, Mary Jane. Don't you want to have lunch with us?" I was so high on cocaine I couldn't get myself out of the room. I responded, "I will meet up with you all later." Soon the front door opened and they left my home. I could hear them chatter as they walked down the outside corridor towards the stairway to the car. Eventually, their voices faded and silence filled my bedroom. I never made it out of my condo that day. I sat undisturbed in a lonely world of addiction, wondering when they would come back knocking at my door. They never did.

My mom weighs in:

Even during those darkest times, Mary Jane managed to hold wonderful jobs. But she began disappearing for longer periods of time. She took my car once to go get coffee, and didn't come back for five days. I had detectives out trying to find her.

She was nominated as one of the top twenty eligible bachelorettes. She was recognized in the Orlando Sentinel. *I mean, amazing stuff. She was scheduled to go on stage where they were doing fundraising, auctioning*

off dates with these beautiful bachelorettes for a charity. It was a huge
event and Mary Jane didn't go! I had no idea why, but I was starting to
suspect that drugs were the reason.

I had originally intended to go to the charity event, of course. It was an honor and I was hugely flattered to be part of it. But I used cocaine that evening and didn't show up for the auction because I was too high. My parents were there in the crowd wondering why their daughter wasn't coming out on stage. I knew in the weeks leading up to this staged and televised event that I wouldn't be able to pull off such a high-profile nomination. Trying on my beautifully designed tea-length, hot pink strapless dress in the days prior to the media interview, I planned how I would escape the performance. As I stood in the mirror watching my designer make alterations to the dress, I would admire his work, while deep down I was terrified. Yet, I smiled approvingly as he made the changes.

The irony is there was a side of me that *was* an accomplished, talented, community driven bachelorette up to the call of being nominated. However, there was also a darker side of my image hiding behind the smiles, struggling to stay alive. My prophecy fulfilled itself; I called the event director and told him I was very ill with a virus. He was disappointed and surprised, of course. Looking back just days after the fiasco, I deeply regretted my behavior, resenting who I was becoming despite my dreams of being useful in the community and successful in my field.

My drug habit was horribly expensive, which didn't escape notice. Dad commented from time to time, "You make more money than anyone your age but have no money in the bank. How can that be?"

I was down to ninety-eight pounds; cocaine was robbing me of my appetite. Living a lie was becoming more and more challenging due to my physical appearance, and I knew it was time to finally admit what was going on.

Driving to my parents' house on a Saturday afternoon, I tried to think of ways to break the news to them. There was no positive spin I could put on the facts, so after a nice lunch of chicken pesto, I just put it out there, bluntly: "Mom, Dad, I think I have a cocaine problem."

Surprisingly, they just kind of shrugged it off. No tears. No drama. It wasn't the reaction I expected. I remember my dad got up from the table and walked into the kitchen as though he missed the entire sentence. My dad said something to the effect of, "Well, don't do it anymore."

He shares his memory:

I didn't know how to respond. That was one of my mistakes, in retrospect. I wish I had done something then. I wish I had said, 'Okay, you're going in for treatment.' I know my response was less than adequate.

Later on, Leigh and I talked about that conversation and it was like we didn't even hear it. It seems silly when you talk about it now. When Mary Jane got even deeper into drugs I thought, 'How could I have been so stupid to not do anything at the time she told us?'

I never knew anything about cocaine. Still to this day, I wouldn't know what it looks like if I saw it. I had no idea but that was a mistake that I made by not being more aggressive with that.

With what felt like a lack of concern from my parents I went out that night and partied. Maybe I was making a bigger deal of it than it was. Maybe my dad was right – I could quit doing coke when I wanted to, easy as that.

So, that night I spent time with friends at a local club where we stood shoulder-to-shoulder among strangers who were also looking for a good time. In public, I smiled. Yet, I felt alone in the world that night after such a dry and unfulfilling conversation with my parents. I had a few drinks that night, but I didn't have the desire to use. I did have the desire to fade away into the background, never to be seen again.

My brother and I were very close during this time in my life. We shared many secrets that gave strength to our bond. He knew my struggle for balance in a chaotic world of drugs, career, and family.

He also stepped in as my protector and went to bat for me on many occasions. His words:

She was my sister. I thought I'd rather have her in the house with me knowing where she was. I could lock the door at night and know where she was. She wasn't out on the streets and I felt I was protecting her better that way.

I was in many, many fights and altercations because of my sister. Seeing the way she was dressed in a bar with guys, I pulled her out of clubs. I got in a lot of fist fights with guys who were disrespecting her... I got my butt kicked many times.

I specifically remember one night in downtown Orlando and Mary Jane was at a club dating some guy I didn't like. I saw the guy push her and I grabbed him. We went toe to toe. That one got broken up by the authorities and we both walked away. Fortunately, we didn't go to jail or anything.

But I've been surrounded by four or five drug dealers and I've had guns pulled on me, all because I was trying to protect Mary Jane.

CHAPTER NINE

Growing up, my brother, dad, mom, and I went to Mass every Sunday. There was no questioning whether or not we would be going that week. It was a given.

When Chad and I were teens, my mom sent us off to church alone. Naturally, we skipped the services and drove around the neighborhood for an hour or two. Then we'd run into the foyer of the church, grab a bulletin, and bring it home as proof of our attendance. My mom even bought that routine a few times.

Once I reached my late twenties, I only attended church on religious holidays, but spent hours and hours writing to God in my journals about my deadly vice and the grip it had on me. I knew I was a drug addict. My therapist, Sally, convinced me of that. But I had no idea how to address my addiction and fix it.

Through writing, I kept reaching out to God. I knew I loved Him. I kept going back in my memory to childhood, recalling how much I adored Jesus when I was little and how I prayed He would sit on my bed and listen to my inner struggles.

It occurred to me that maybe I could find help for my addiction if I went back to church. Through mutual friends, I met a girl named

Liz who invited me to a Community Church, a nondenominational fellowship in Orlando. It was my first charismatic experience, and I immediately took to the worship music and the Pastor's messages. I began attending two or three services a month and always ended up crying my eyes out. Yet, even though the sermons were compelling, drugs exerted a stronger pull.

I couldn't quit using. I waved my hands and sang along to the praise music, really trying to enjoy those beautiful times at church. But I knew when the service was over I would have to go looking for my next high.

When Liz moved, I kept going to this church, even taking a few friends along with me. I often got high on a Saturday night, then went to church (still high) on Sunday morning. I switched, then, to a Saturday afternoon service so I could focus on the sermon.

I sat in the back of the church where it was easier to cry without being noticed. I would listen to the message and agree with everything the Pastor said, but it was like a flesh-versus-spirit thing. My spirit knew that what I was doing was unhealthy and wrong and dangerous, but the flesh couldn't stop. Ironically, the church was only blocks from my dealer's house in "the 'hood." Because I was in the fight of my life, I went to church expecting a supernatural healing. When God didn't deliver my holy and immediate healing each week, I would go from church to Eric, my dealer, and pick up dope. It felt like a tug-of-war inside me pulling in each direction: life verses death. I was growing resentful of this God who knew I was desperate for a miracle and still wasn't performing like the Pastor promised He could.

I didn't want to be an addict. I wanted to be in a great relationship, and have kids, and a terrific job, and a stellar relationship with my family. I wanted to experience the kind of contentment and happiness I saw friends enjoying. I didn't want to fear what kind of trouble my Saturday nights would bring after leaving the safety of God's house.

Along the way, through mutual acquaintances and deadbeat addicts, I met a guy named L.J. who fit the image of a stereotypical drug user – dark greasy hair, messed-up teeth, drove a beat-up Camaro. L.J. was the nicest guy in the world and didn't want me "out there" looking for drugs, so he brought them to me in an attempt to keep me safe. L.J. and I would travel about the city in his Camaro visiting his friends. Once, L.J. left me alone with a stranger and promised he would return within 60 minutes. Several hours later, I took this stranger's truck in attempt to find my apartment. I was fed up with L.J. and I was determined to go home! I didn't recognize the street names or the area. I drove aimlessly, ending up on a dirt road until I pulled up to a random house, walked through the side door where a family was eating lunch, and ask them to help me find my way home. Strangely, they didn't seem afraid of me. Like guardian angels, they gave me direction toward my condo, which I followed until a police officer pulled me over. Again, blessed with God's grace, the officer asked me where I was headed and offered me direction. Oddly, he didn't seem to notice my disheveled appearance, and inability to find my way home. I was once again home safe without causing harm to anyone.

This incident is one more amazing example of how I was given extreme grace, and not what I deserved. In reality, I could've been arrested for DUI and taken to jail. I was utterly exhausted from the late night and driving dangerously through neighborhoods I couldn't find, even today. This important sequence of events served as a reminder to me that my guardian angel was making a way for me to recover, get home safely on most days, and that God was always on my side.

When I went to my dealer, I usually bought a gram or two of cocaine for about $160 which would last me several days. I heard about people who could do an "eight ball" (around three–and- a-half grams of coke) in one night, but that scared the life out of me. I was afraid my heart would stop if I did that much. My mind was occupied enough with thoughts of getting caught: *What do I do if the phone rings? What do I do if someone knocks on the door?* I was always planning my escape.

I had gone from a happy-go-lucky young woman with those nine party girls to a paranoid cocaine user. I cut out using Ecstasy, but now felt alone in my much deeper, darker addiction to lines of white powder. I did it late at night when the house was dark. My brother was downstairs sleeping and I was upstairs doing a line of cocaine by myself.

Lying in bed, I thought about how different my life would be if I had married Mitch the cop. *Where would I be if I had just gone through with that marriage, if I hadn't let him get away?* I felt like I was going through spiritual hell. Just like one can become healthy, fit, and strong by shedding weight, the opposite can happen. I was adding on pounds of sin to my life. Sin, defined as *"missing the mark"* described my recent life experience. The weight of who I had become was a heavy burden laden with fear, poor health, mental strain, and the need for treatment. By now, I was a burden to anyone who loved me or cared about me. I was stealing their peace of mind, as well as material items. I was not able to show up for my job and constantly called in sick to work. I was unable to show up for family gatherings. I was lying and becoming the stereotypical junkie. The contrast, between whom I dreamed of becoming as a little girl and who I became in reality, was so drastic that I could hardly wake up each morning, open my eyes, lift myself off the pillow, and start my day. I would look in the mirror and ask myself, *Mary Jane, how did you get to this point?*

One night I began to fear I would die. I thought, *if my family gets a call that I've passed away, would they ever know how much I loved them?* I wanted them to understand that even in my toughest days alone, I thought about them all the time.

This letter was written when it was most quiet in the wee hours after midnight. That was the time of day I hated the most. I turned on the

TV to fill the silence. I drank a cold beer while I wrote this suicide note, taking deep breaths to calm my nerves.

～

Dear family,

A sudden urge came over me as I was lying down. Because I am an addict who has had a difficult time staying sober, there is always a chance that my heart will decide it's had enough. If you find this, I am with Jesus creating each sunrise and sunset for you to remember me by. You all love to walk the beach and every time you absorb the sun, we will be together spiritually. Every afternoon you spend at Disappearing Island, you'll feel my touch as you lay in the waves. Every holiday you gather together, the sound of my laughter will echo with yours. And every time you face a challenge that brings you to your knees, I will be there praying with you.

I've tried so many times to get my life back on track. I've just grown tired, so very tired of fighting this intense craving. It's hard to explain the emptiness I feel. My addiction has taken all of my God-gifted passions to the point I feel nothing, really. Except fear! I feel a lot of that.

You have walked through my journey with me. I just needed to tell you all how much I love you and how grateful I am for all your love, prayers, and commitment to my life. I hope you never see this letter but I couldn't leave without saying "I'll see you in Heaven!"

Please forgive me for stealing your peace of mind and causing you pain and worry.

I love you so much,

Mary Jane

～

CHAPTER TEN

For my job at Dekko's Night Club, I threw a big party with a thousand guests when the club partnered with an adult contemporary radio station that played Top 40 hits. A woman from the station saw the work I was doing, and was impressed by my salesmanship and marketing ideas. She pulled me aside one day and said, "If you ever want to get out of this and come to work with me, let me know." Two weeks later, I started working in radio sales with Linda. I left Dekko's so easily because Linda was a remarkable business woman -- and I wanted a new career.

I excelled at selling radio ads, hunting down some of the biggest and most prestigious accounts in Orlando. Besides the money, which was three times more than I was making at Dekko's, there were other perks to my new job. I was like a little girl in a candy store, getting all the free tickets to the hottest events. Want to go to the sold-out Janet Jackson concert? I was your girl. Need a free pass to Disney World, or exclusive VIP tickets to a private club? I got it without even breaking a nail. I was the girl who could get you in anywhere. All the velvet ropes lifted when I arrived on the scene.

I set up promotions for a lot of huge concerts: The Dave Matthews Band, The Real McCoy, Fiona Apple, and Hootie and the Blowfish, to name a few. I worked with Shaquille O'Neal and Snoop Dogg when they shot music videos in town. I worked with these celebrities and many more, maintaining a professional façade at work by creating dynamic events, exceeding my sales goals, and establishing strong clientele relationships. My old party friends, however, still sensed that my personal life was spiraling. One night I shared a drink with Allison. She was blunt: "Mary Jane, you are way too thin. I'm really worried about you. I think you need some help." The absurdity of her confrontation struck me: Allison was the catalyst who introduced me to the nine party girls, putting me on the road to addiction in the first place. But unlike me, Allison controlled her habit. I was barely able to keep my destructive personal life from seeping into my professional one.

My job did nothing to curb my drug habit. Like many other people, I also worked 9 to 5, but my hours were 9:00 p.m. to 5:00 a.m., and my office was whatever bar, club, or concert my client's heart desired. I was getting paid to book advertising, attend parties, and entertain celebrities.

Over time, my frail composure became apparent to my new bosses. Called into the office, my employers told me they didn't want me doing nightclub events anymore because they thought I was burning the candle at both ends. They could see I was getting into trouble doing those events. "You'll keep all the big accounts, like Disney and Blockbuster, but maybe you shouldn't have to go to all these gigs."

They all chose their words carefully but I knew they were onto my shameful secrets. I was losing control of my behavior. I was becoming more unpredictable. I had lost a tremendous amount of weight and my "All-American" style was diminishing. I could no longer live two lives.

Through my hairdresser, I met two brothers named Billy and Jordan. Billy owned the salon and Jordan ran a shoe store. Jordan was also a drug dealer who started supplying my "fix." We became friends. It was utterly platonic because although I enjoyed going to the movies and meeting him for a meal, Jordan was nothing to look at. But Jordan's appeal was unique. He was charming and understated. His preference was to blend into a room instead of attracting attention. I was drawn to him because he was mysterious and disciplined. I remember meeting him at a nice restaurant for a drug exchange. We decided to share dinner first and I remember people looking at us with curious expressions that said: *Why are these two people having dinner together?*

We didn't look like a good match, but I knew on the inside there were no differences between us. I wasn't going to judge him or anybody else because I had my own cross to bear. I knew all addicts, regardless of what we look like on the outside, are fighting the same spiritual battle for our souls and our salvation. For me to judge would be hypocritical.

One night over seafood, Jordan casually told me he was headed out of town to buy a kilo of cocaine. I didn't have much of a reaction. *What did I care? Good for him.* After seafood, we went to a Queen Latifah movie and had a great time laughing our heads off while completely sober.

Jordan seemed to care for me, outside of selling me drugs. In a strange way, we were friends. At one point I was looking pretty haggard, so he suggested I lay off the coke for a little while. I was paper thin-due to late-night partying and a heavy work load. I took his advice for the next few weeks and tried to chill out, stay sober, and focus on my job.

Later that month, I was ready for another gram or two of coke. I had been clean for a few weeks and I looked healthier. My work improved, but my so-called sobriety was really becoming precarious. I headed back to the shoe store to make a purchase. When I arrived, Jordan grabbed my arm painfully and pulled me to the shoe stockroom. His sudden violence and intensity shocked me.

"Where have you been?" Jordan barked.

"Nowhere. I haven't been using for a few weeks, but that's it. You're the one who told me to chill out for a while because I was getting too much coke and losing too much weight."

"I don't believe you. My house got raided," he hissed. "I just think it's a little too coincidental that you've been gone and my house gets raided. Did you tell the police?"

I had no idea what he was talking about. There was no way I would have reported him to the police. For starters, I was afraid of the cops, which was ironic since I almost married one before the drugs got really bad. Besides, I had my own illegal substance abuse to hide. Secondly, Jordan was my dealer and it would make no sense for me to rat him out.

Then Jordan's brother, Billy, arrived and got involved in the accusations "You must have told your acquaintances or your friends," he insisted. "You told somebody. Who did you tell?"

I promised Jordan and Billy I hadn't spoken to anyone about either of them. They didn't believe me.

"One of three options," Jordan threatened, getting in my face and pressing me up against the stone wall. "You'll be sitting at dinner having a glass of wine with your girlfriends and I'll send someone to beat you within an inch of your life. Option two, you'll be on the run for the rest of your life and will sleep with one eye open. Three, you might just die."

I was terrified by their threats. It felt like the Mafia had put a hit out on me. I was still in grave danger as we approached the Thanksgiving holiday, and stripped of my peace of mind during Christmas. Alone, I wept over my situation, too terrified to tell anyone. On New Year's Eve, my boyfriend was going to stay over at my place but we got into a fight.

I had picked him up earlier in the evening, and we went to a themed party. I didn't have any intention of driving him back home after the argument we had about his flirting with my one of my girlfriends. I just told him to take my car home and return it in the morning when things cooled off.

He left my condo, and I was alone again. My brother was away that evening on a trip to Chicago. At one-thirty in the morning, I was doing coke in Chad's room watching television; I didn't like being by myself overnight, and staying downstairs felt safer. Suddenly, I heard something outside. I wasn't sure if I was jittery from the coke or if I had really heard a noise. We lived in a pretty busy apartment complex and people often got home from work late. Plus, it was New Year's Eve so there was a lot going on outside.

Peeking out the front window I could see a man leaning against a tree in front of my condo, staring at my front door. I jumped, remembering Jordan's threat last month.

I ran to the second floor to confirm it wasn't the drugs tweaking me out. There he stood, a frightening figure of a man leaning by the tree. I can remember his white T-shirt, blue jeans, and long brown hair.

Oh no, this is the guy Jordan sent, I thought and sprinted downstairs. Panic set in immediately; the day Jordan threatened had finally come. This would be my death and how I would be remembered. My heart was beating like a drum and I could hear the tempo pounding inside my eardrums. My palms began to sweat as I frantically paced the floor deciding what to do. I had never shot a gun, but knew Chad kept one for protection. I grabbed it from underneath Chad's mattress. It was a .38 revolver.

The front door was locked but I heard our screen door open. I stood behind the door, shaking, gun to my side. I saw the door handle turn slowly to the right and then slowly to the left, like a scene from a horror film. Suddenly, the doorknob began racing back and forth as he tried to get into my condo. Then a huge thump rang out, and the next thing I knew, a gun went off. I assumed the intruder had shot at our door handle trying to explode the lock.

I smelled gunpowder and wondered how the scent was getting inside. The door knob stopped turning and I heard the man elbow the screen door aside and run off.

I looked for a bullet hole in the door and found nothing. Stepping off the stairs, I fell to the ground. That's when it hit me, literally and figuratively. I had shot myself in the leg.

I hadn't felt the pain. Maybe it was the fear or adrenaline or my pounding heart, but I never felt the bullet go in. I looked down at my pink Victoria's Secrets pajamas and there was a huge hole in right pant leg. The bullet missed my right knee cap by less than a quarter of an inch, burying itself in my thigh.

Obviously my finger was on the trigger. I never held a gun before that night, and had no idea it was even cocked. Realizing what I had done to myself, the thought flashed through my mind, *What??? I'm Mary Jane. This doesn't happen to me! I am a Homecoming Queen. I make eighty grand a year and drive a Mazda RX7! I am a local celebrity!* I could see myself sitting on the bottom stair as I had an out-of-body experience.

I stumbled over to the unit of my next door neighbor, a retired police officer. As I bled all over his front porch, he said he didn't want to help me. He heard the gunshot and didn't want any part of it.

I limped back to my condo and wrapped my leg in a towel. I needed to call 911, but first I would have to destroy the drugs. If I didn't throw out the cocaine I would be arrested.

While I was on the phone with emergency response, I took my bag of coke and flushed it. "I just suffered a gunshot wound. Someone was trying to break into my house," I said. Minutes later the police and paramedics arrived. The cops searched around and made sure there wasn't anyone else hiding in the condo. I held my breath, watching them open closet doors and cabinet drawers. I was more upset about the gram of coke I flushed than the quarts of blood I lost.

The paramedics carried me out on a gurney. At the hospital, police officers continued to drill me with inquires. I told them the truth, that I shot myself by accident trying to protect myself from an intruder. I have no idea if the officers knew I was high on coke during the interrogation. They kept saying my name to get me to sit up and talk. But, horrified and alone in the emergency room, I pretended to be asleep although I could hear them talking to me, asking me for information. However, I knew I was still in serious danger and wasn't about to share any information about Jordan or the threats on my life.

If there's such a thing as a naïve drug user, it was me. I never thought through the concept of people making drugs or selling them. I didn't know what trafficking was and didn't comprehend the danger I was in. The mechanics behind how drugs arrived in my lap never registered with me. I didn't care.

I got my drugs at an upscale hair salon. I walked in, got my hair done for Saturday night, and exchanged cash for drugs in the stock room. I still existed in a world where people drove Lexus cars and lived in beautiful homes on gorgeous Florida waterfronts.

It was soon revealed that Jordan's nephew had been pulled over that November, in possession of some pretty serious drugs including cocaine and Ecstasy. This nephew made a deal with law enforcement. In exchange for wearing a wire, they promised to reduce his sentence -- which is how he became part of a sting operation against Jordan.

When the brothers finally learned the truth, Jordan called me at the radio station.

"Will you forgive me?" he asked. "I found out it was my nephew. I thought it was you the whole time."

"Did you send someone to my house?" I asked, pointedly.

The line went silent. Jordan took a few moments and muttered, "I hope you can forgive me."

"This is the last time we can ever speak to one another," I muttered before hanging up the phone. We never spoke or crossed paths again.

My mind was whirling with thoughts about how I got to this point: my leg propped up in a cast from a self-inflicted gunshot wound that occurred trying to protect myself from someone sent by my drug dealer to beat me up or worse.

CHAPTER ELEVEN

Just like some of the chapters of my life (and this book), this one begins with a man.

Jake was one of the best things to happen to me for a while. He was a handsome, six-foot-three volleyball player with brown hair, blue eyes, and a brilliant mind. He loved music, motorcycles, and politics, yet was soft spoken. Despite my "issues," we had a really healthy relationship. He kept me as grounded as possible and left me in good spirits. Jake showed me what living a clean life could actually be like.

We met at a trendy nightclub. After exchanging glances all night, he finally walked up to me and asked me to dance. We enjoyed the evening getting to know one another. At closing, he took my number.

Once we celebrated a year of dating, we moved in together. Following my self-inflicted gunshot wound, it was nice to have someone around to protect me...even from myself. Jake had a great job in pharmaceuticals, and we spent picture-perfect weekends going motorcycle riding, inviting friends over to the pool, playing volleyball, barbecuing, and taking out the wave runners.

I felt rather free. I was hanging out with healthy people. Jake only drank beer and my drug use was at a minimum. The drama of the gunshot had really scared me straight.

That spring, we went on a fantastic skiing trip in Colorado. At first I didn't know if I would be able to go, since I wasn't sure how extensive the damage from the bullet might still be. My doctor finally cleared me to go. It felt so good to get out of Central Florida with Jake and his childhood friends to a place where nobody knew me. I felt a sense of freedom -- and a new beginning.

When I was with Jake, I felt healthier, safer, and more protected than I had in years. But it wasn't all perfect. We had our spiritual differences; he was Jewish and I was a Christian. Jake promised his grandfather, a Holocaust survivor, he would carry on the legacy of Judaism. But religious differences were not the issue that drove us apart; my substance abuse problem was the more pressing issue at hand. A little drug use turned into more and more drug use.

Unfortunately, the drug habit I naively believed I had "under control" once again reared its ugly head. Hiding my use caused an uncomfortable, haunting tension within my soul that followed me everywhere. I didn't trust myself. I wasn't treating the illness by going to meetings or to therapy. I was using healthy people as a bandage to cover my open wound.

But that bandage was suddenly ripped away when Jake broke up with me. I wish I remembered more about what transpired, but I can only recall that I experienced some kind of spiraling-down episode that ended the relationship. Jake realized the contrast and gap between us was too great. He told me, "I love you Mary Jane, and I always will, but I'm scared of your drug habit. I wish I could help you, but I can't. I just can't." I remember exactly where I was standing inside my parents' home that summer afternoon when Jake said those words. I was devastated -- heartbroken over the end of our love affair, and also inconsolable about the loss of our friendship. To me, Jake wasn't just my boyfriend, he was my best friend. It's probably one of the greatest friendship losses I have ever suffered. He was such a beautiful human being.

I moved back into the safety of my parents' house, but soon began hanging out with more dangerous people without Jake to anchor me. I wasn't making it to the radio station every day. People at work knew something was terribly wrong and were pulling me aside, coaching me on what to tell the boss, trying to save my job -- and me. A popular DJ walked me to my car one night and physically shook me, saying, "No more! This is it. No more cocaine for you. This is ridiculous. You're gonna kill yourself!"

Though I was holding on by my fingernails to this glamorous, lucrative job, one disastrous gig ended my once-promising and illustrious career in radio. I organized celebrity appearances to do promotions, inviting some of our biggest clients (mainly Disney and Miller Brewing Company) to meet-and-greet the talent. A lot was riding on the success of this event: not only my job and professional reputation, but hundreds of thousands of dollars in advertising for our station.

Yet, there I sat on a tattered green couch, already an hour late for the event. My drug-buddy reminded me that if I called my dealer and spent my last $100, the career I loved would be over. I picked up my cell phone anyway, and ordered more drugs for delivery. Looking back, I didn't feel regret about the inevitable loss of my job, but rather an overwhelming sense of relief. My exhausting charade was over.

The night I didn't show up at the event, I left one of my co-workers to entertain my professional guests. Of course my boss called my cell phone. When I didn't answer, she called my mom and asked if I was on my way.

"I'm not sure," my mom said.

"It's over for Mary Jane," was my boss's reply before she hung up.

I left her no choice but to fire me. Like my ex-boyfriend Jake, my boss knew I was a lost cause. She told me, "Girl, it's not because I don't love you, it's because I can't keep you."

I had lost my $80,000-a-year job, my exciting career, and my VIP status. Oddly, I felt free. I was so glad I didn't have to fake it anymore. No more getting dressed in the morning, putting on a suit, driving a fancy car, pretending I was okay while privately fighting a battle with drugs at night. It was a relief to just be an addict and not have to pretend to be something I wasn't.

My mom:

I recall driving her over to the radio station to pick up her last check. She didn't have her car due to drugs or something. Her license was probably suspended. Mary Jane went in, picked up her stuff, and got back in the car without so much as a word.

All I could think was, You were number one! And you lost it. *But I didn't say that to her. There was just silence in the car between us.*

CHAPTER TWELVE

It was an absolutely wonderful night on the dance floor. I knew I looked hot in my white hip huggers, tight tank top, and platform shoes. It was the late Nineties and to some degree, Seventies fashion had been reborn. I was having my own little Studio 54 moment several decades later.

I arrived home to find the condo I shared with a roommate filled with scary looking strangers. *What kind of drug addicts are these?* I asked myself in a moment of judgment. I was high on Ecstasy and wasn't in the mood for all these strung-out deadbeats in my house.

My roommate and his buddy Shane came in from the kitchen. "Hey Mary Jane, you gotta try this new thing," Shane said, sounding like a line of dialogue stolen from an *Afterschool Special.* Because I was intoxicated, my inhibitions were down so I followed them into the kitchen. On the counter sat a crushed Coke can with cigarette ashes on top, specks of white dust sprinkled within those ashes. Shane picked me up, placed me on the counter, and fired up the lighter. He told me to slowly inhale the smoke inside the can.

I didn't ask questions, I just inhaled. Moments later there was a sense of excitement rushing through my veins, altering my state like flipping a light switch, taking me from complete relaxation to an intense adrenalin rush. It was powerful, but I still wasn't so sure I liked it. I felt totally awake, hyper-alert, and instantly fearful the cops were on their way.

I walked upstairs and decided whatever that was, it wasn't for me. Furthermore, I wanted these dirty looking people out of my house. It felt like they all had a hard edge to them. I walked into my room to find a couple of girls in my bathroom. "What's going on?" I snapped. "Get out of here."

I stormed back downstairs to tell my roommate I was fed up. In the kitchen there were more crushed soda cans on the counter. "Shane, why do you have four or five ashtrays going with all these cigarettes? You're not even smoking them." He explained that they were collecting the soot of the cigarettes. They put the soot on the can, along with some crack cocaine, and smoked it. This was my introduction to crack.

My roommate explains more:

I think that was the first time she tried it. It was pretty intense. She leaned back on the counter and kept saying, "Wow, wow. Incredible."

I felt something in my gut saying this was bad. I had done it many times before that night and I knew that it's an ugly drug. Crack is like a python gripping your neck. It creates a very euphoric feeling in your head. When you exhale, that's when you have the most feeling in your brain. A very short time later, it's gone and you want more. It's a very short high.

I can't believe I introduced her to the drug. It's one of those things -- when you turn it on, it's tough to turn off. I take a lot of responsibility for that.

I mean, would she have tried it somewhere else? I can't say yes; I can't say no. She tried it that night and that's what created it. That's what lit the fire. This started the spiral down -- the demon, the Devil.

Crack is different from the powder to which I was accustomed; while both are forms of cocaine, crack is formed into solid "rocks" and smoked, getting you high much quicker. That night it took me someplace I had never been before. The high was so much higher, more intense than anything I had ever before experienced. Instantaneously, my mind soared. I became acutely aware that I was no longer able to make rational decisions. It felt too powerful, like all the nerves in my skin were exposed to a supernatural world beyond simple human conception. I felt invincible.

Looking back, I wish I had never tried crack that night. It began the years of desperation and a willingness on my part to do whatever it took to get high. I began stealing from my own brother to pay for the drugs.

He recalls:

I got so tired of her stealing from me: my watches, my wallet, my car, PlayStations, TVs, radios – if she could pawn it, she would. Now granted, if I had a party and eight or ten of my CDs were missing, that could have been because I had a bunch of drug-heads in my house. But they weren't walking out with important, expensive stuff.

Mary Jane knew where my checkbook was and she would go sixteen checks in and rip out a blank one so I couldn't tell it was missing. My account would then be two hundred dollars in the negative because she was writing checks for drugs. She denied it. "It wasn't me" she always claimed. It was never her.

I moved out of the drug den/condo and back into my folks' house yet again, and began stealing from them: cell phones, stuff of value from the garage, or anything else I could find.

On Valentine's Day, my dad surprised my mom with a one-and–a-half-carat diamond necklace. She loved the thoughtful gift and went on and on about it. I, on the other hand, was careful to notice where she put the necklace -- in her jewelry box in her bedroom.

They went out for dinner later that night and all I could think about was that necklace. I knew if I stole it I would get caught, but I needed the drugs so badly. It felt like my body was going through withdrawal. I didn't think through my actions that night. I was so empty. It didn't even register how badly this betrayal would hurt my mom. I was a walking dead person – a one-hundred-pound, frail young woman who rarely ate or slept.

While they were out, I snatched the diamond from my parents' room and held it in my pocket. When Mom arrived home, she went to her bedroom to take off her jewelry and immediately knew her expensive gift was gone. She charged out to the living room and demanded to know where it was. I sat on the couch, watching TV. With blank expression on my face I said, "I don't know what you're talking about."

"Mary Jane, just tell me what you did with it. I'll go get it. Dad bought me this," she pressed.

I shrugged.

My dad took over. "Look, your mom is really upset. Just tell me what pawn shop." I looked him in the eye and lied to his face without even flinching -- all with the diamond necklace in my pocket.

The next day I pawned it for $200, which helped me purchase more crack. For days I continued to brush off my mom's accusations. Until then, things I took were not of great sentimental value – but now I'd crossed a line. That necklace was important to her, financially and emotionally, and I took it. It's not like my father had money to throw around. This was probably something he saved for over many months, and my mom knew for a fact I stole it.

My conscience played out like the cartoon angel and devil on my shoulders. Despite my addiction, there was still a consciousness of right and wrong. The last thing I wanted to do was hurt my family. I knew I needed to admit what I had done, and I finally told my dad that I had taken it.

"Just tell me where it is and I'll give them the money to get it back," he said with an exasperated sigh. The next day he and I visited the pawn shop but the necklace was gone, already sold. Even in my state of mind, I knew this was a crushing blow to our relationship. My addiction had hit a horrible new milestone.

When we arrived home from the pawn shop, I found my belongings packed in trash bags on the front doorstep. My mom had enough of her own daughter.

CHAPTER THIRTEEN

Because of my blatant lying and stealing from my parents, to say things had become strained between us would be an understatement. It's only fair to let them share their side of the story. My mom begins:

Things had gotten so horrible. She looked like a maniac. Her hair was pulled back, her face was drawn in. I got to the point I had to let her go. Mary Jane wasn't happy with my decision to pack her bags. She followed me around the house screaming that I was a ... let's just say... "not-nice person."

Joe didn't agree with my decision, so he found himself a chair and waited it out. I ran outside but she followed me. I'm just glad she didn't have a weapon. I knew she was over the deep end and needed to be locked up. I didn't want my daughter in prison but I knew she was a danger to herself. My heart was broken to see my daughter in such a dreadful state of mind and yet I was relieved to see her go.

After she left, I went back in the house and cried. I was so angry with Joe. He just could not deal with it.

My dad shares his side:

Leigh and I love each other a lot. We decided we couldn't let what was happening take that away from us. Leigh kind of "sacrificed" Mary Jane by putting her belongings on the porch that night. She realized she couldn't do anything more for her right then.

We talked about it all the time, day after day after day. The stress was unbelievably exhausting. I don't know that we ever sat down and said, "We either give up Mary Jane or our marriage is over with." I don't remember it ever getting to that point. But I do remember so many conversations about the stress and the strain we were having. We were worried we would get that call that our daughter was dead on the street, someplace. All we could do was ask for God's help.

My mom:

I'd be on the beach on a beautiful day, calling out for Mary Jane in my prayers, not knowing where she was. She went from age twenty-five to thirty and lost half a decade. She has few memories of it. She tells me she really missed some of the best youthful years of her life, and she believes the greatest cost was not having her own children.

By the time I kicked her out, she had lost everything -- all sense of feeling, all of her joy. Drugs do that to you. They take everything from you.

From that time on Mary Jane and I totally disconnected. Joe became her safety line. He worked overtime so he could pay her rent, buy her groceries, whatever. Mary Jane would talk only to her Dad on the phone. She and I weren't speaking. I never told Joe I didn't want him seeing our daughter but I wanted him doing it in his own time. He took over and showed love to her. I was able to have a little freedom. I was done and worn out and my Mom was real sick. It's a miracle our marriage survived.

My dad:

I didn't want Leigh to be worried about Mary Jane and I believed it was my turn. Leigh had the guts to kick her out and I wanted to help bring her back around.

Mary Jane called the house from time to time and I would take her out for breakfast or lunch. She was Daddy's little girl. The man is supposed to do these things, so I took her out to Publix and bought her groceries and made sure she had food to eat. Then maybe we wouldn't talk for a week or two before she'd call again. I never gave her money but I would go get food with her. I didn't want to be an enabler but I didn't want her to starve to death or turn to the streets to support her habit.

I gave her a car because she had no transportation. I knew she was using that car to move from place to place. She had many roommates during that time and I just didn't want her out on the street. That was my way. When days went by without a word, I went out looking for her and drove around for hours looking for her car in the kind of neighborhoods that you go out of your way to avoid.

I didn't want Leigh to hurt, to feel the pain. I would rather have the pain than her feel it. When I took Mary Jane to get groceries, at least I could come back and tell Leigh that our daughter was alive. I didn't give her a lot of details about how she looked or whatever – just the basic, positive highlights. Not that there were many positives.

I was always praying that God would give me the strength to do what I had to do. I just couldn't let her go.

I asked my dad about my mom all the time. I missed her but understood to some degree why I was cut out of her life. Dad gave me the basics: "Mom's doing okay; you know she loves you," but that was about it. His loyalty was to his wife and he was stuck in the middle between the two of us.

One day I turned to him in desperation and said, "Dad, this is a spiritual battle between the enemy and me. I am in the fight of my life right now and the Devil would rather me die than live. You're the spiritual leader of the home. You can't let go of me now because I'm in such a dark hole. If you and Mom quit praying for me, I will die."

We all knew that it was spiritual. My dad promised to never give up on me and we clung to one another. One of the few times my mom came with my dad, I was bawling and both my parents were sobbing as we embraced. My drug addiction was so much bigger than me and I didn't know how to stop it. As embarrassing as it was for me to have my father see me like that, that conversation kept me alive. The Devil wanted me dead and the human body can only take so much. Somehow, I knew this was a battle for my life and my sanity. Without the spiritual protection of my parents, I would fade into oblivion.

One lonely night, I wrote this letter to myself:

As I sit at the computer I am forced to be honest with myself about the pain I feel today. For the last few days I have been walking past this computer, sitting down, finding myself unable to put my feelings into words. I'm not sure if it's fear of the truth I can't handle or if I am still trying to figure out what I feel. All I know is I cannot sleep regularly and my appetite is practically gone. I have lost my job and my family in a matter of a year and I am so alone.

Or at least I feel that way. I know that God is here because I feel Him close to me. He wants me to face this pain, but not completely alone. My whole life my family has never validated any suffering. The theory of my family is to ignore it and it will eventually go away. I must admit that I, too, have tried to ignore my pain and it didn't go away. Maybe it eased up from time to time but it always shows its face when I least expect it. And it always knocks me off my feet and I lose.

I don't even know how to deal with the heartache I am experiencing. I feel sick to my stomach. It's been hard to eat and hard to sleep all the way through the night. I begin to cry until the tears stop. It's almost like I am beyond the pain of tears.

Mom and Dad have turned their backs on me. Three times I have asked (in desperate tears) to get into a thirty-day program to kick the so-called "habit" that has disrupted my life. I guess the Lord is telling me that this is a journey I must travel without my parents. Why? I'm not sure.

However, I know that I want to lead a drug-free life where I can be a servant leader to spread God's Word. If I have to do it without the support of my immediate family, I will. I will take responsibility for my actions and I will accomplish this task ahead by asking God to speak to me. I will do my best to keep my ears and mind open to hearing Him. That is key. My mind is full of thoughts, yet I can't seem to focus my words. Right now they feel more like emotions than words. Cluttered and mixed up with so many feelings…

Obviously my drug haze clouded the vision of my family. They had done so much for me. Chad, the little brother who used to idolize his sister, had rescued me over and over again. I'll let him share his side:

One night I knew she was laid up in a motel somewhere. I knew of a couple locations she would probably be and I eventually found her car in a parking lot. I walked around the complex, trying to find her.

When I knocked on her door a drug dealer answered it. I froze in my tracks. "Where's my sister?" I asked.

"Your bleeping sister wrote us a bad check and when I meet up with her, I'm gonna hurt her," he said through clenched teeth. Apparently, Mary Jane had traded her car for drugs, which explained why it was parked out front. Dealers were always looking for new vehicles since they delivered drugs to the same clientele over and over. Because they were worried about being followed by the cops, they'd use someone's red car then switch it up the next week with someone else's white car.

With a gun in his hand, the dealer told me how much my sister owed him. I promised him I'd get him cash and I did, right away. He exchanged her bounced check for the cash and told me to get out of there.

Mary Jane called me up all the time and I always agreed to get her. I didn't care where she was. One night she was in a little scumbag motel and she got scared. She was in her room where she had probably been for days and heard a noise.

Frightened, she ran to the lobby and begged the pregnant woman behind the desk not to call the cops. She called me, crying and paranoid. I had to show up and convince her that it was okay. When I pulled up, the police were there talking to her and the front desk clerk and asking her about the carload of drug dealers that were looking for her. They wanted to know why. She was terrified to say anything and eventually I got to see her up close. But just to see her face all drawn in. She was as thin as paper. You could see her fingertips were black and torn apart from the crack pipe. All I could do at that point was get her home, tuck her into bed, and lock the door.

I rarely told my parents about these incidents. I tried to protect them from more hurt. I wanted harmony. I saw them fighting all the time and not talking to each other. I felt like my dad was drinking heavily. My mom was gone emotionally, always in tears, very depressed. What hurt me most was watching the deterioration of my parents. My heart absolutely broke for my sister, but to see my parents go through it – that crushed me.

I just wanted Mary Jane out of my life at that point. I wished she had never been born, or at least wanted to see her hauled off to jail -- whatever it took for us to start the healing process.

CHAPTER FOURTEEN

Drugs destroyed my life. My fancy Mazda RX7 was repossessed and I was driving an older car, 1983 Pontiac my dad gave me. Because I had no job and no money, that car became my only currency for getting crack by lending it to drug dealers for periods of time – sometimes hours, sometimes days. These guys were always looking for a new vehicle so they could make their regular deliveries and remain undetected by the cops.

But this arrangement came with a price. Often the car was returned to me completely trashed. One dealer drove my vehicle through a neighborhood and someone who didn't like him took a baseball bat to my windshield. But what could I do about it? These were scary people. I still had memories of the thug sent by Jordan who tried to break into my place which resulted in a gunshot wound.

Eric, who lived near the church I once attended, was still my crack dealer. He was protective of me -- as protective as a drug pusher could be. Because he didn't want to see me in the more dangerous neighborhoods, I got the drugs by going directly to his house. Sometimes, he and his girlfriend let me stay at their place because they were worried about me. He was looking at a once upper-middle-class, college-educated, successfully employed former Homecoming Queen who was in over her head. He would earnestly plead with me to get help, go home, stop calling, quit knocking on his door, and stay away from the dangerous neighborhoods that produced some of Orlando's most dangerous criminals. Yet, because I was desperate to stay on the destructive path of drug use, he continued to supply me with crack cocaine. His girlfriend, Mauve, would quietly pull me aside to share her concerns that one day I would die of overdose, or that I would be a victim in a crime. Yet, I ignored her genuine desire to help me see the truth about myself and the grave danger I was putting myself in.

One night I drove over to Eric's, but he wasn't home. The backseat of my car was covered with drug recovery literature and workbooks. I was going to 12-Step meetings, but a meeting is only as good as what you do outside of it -- and I was still smoking crack every day.

Without drugs in my system, I would withdraw, becoming unstable and insecure. My mind would short circuit, becoming completely focused on getting more drugs. It felt like starvation from food; a deep and consuming hunger, only for a chemical fix. Extreme anxiety would overwhelm my aching body and panic would overtake my mind. I knew the only way I would feel normal again would be to inhale more smoke from my crack pipe. Desperate for a fix, I drove to the most notorious neighborhood in Orlando; my only fear wasn't for my life or my material possessions, but that I wouldn't be able to find more crack.

I was driving around a bad neighborhood and eventually I pulled up to a crack house where a beautiful black woman was standing in the front door. She had gorgeous long black curly hair, loosely hanging around her shoulders, and pearly white teeth. Though she was plainly dressed in low-riding jeans and a simple white T-shirt, her outer beauty invited me to trust her immediately. "Hi," I leaned out my car window and said, "I'm looking for Eric."

She told me he wasn't there at the moment but she would be glad to help me. Tina must have sensed I had some money in my pocket because she invited me to come in for a while and party. I *knew better* than to go inside, but I did it anyway.

For a half-hour or so things were fine. She invited me into a room, locked the door behind me, and we sat cross-legged on the floor facing one another while we got high. Without asking me for money, she offered me a few hits while we made small talk. I felt relatively safe at that time. Then, Tina asked if she could borrow my car to go find some more drugs. I hesitated because of the past trouble loaning out my car, and that's when the violence began. Tina went crazy. She was a lot bigger than me, as I stood 5 feet 2 inches and weighed 110 pounds while she was at least 5 feet. 6 inches and weighed approximately 150 pounds. I could feel her strength as she threw me up against a wall, banging my head against a large framed picture. Before I could catch my breath and figure out what just happened. Tina forcefully pinned my shoulders against the wall, thrusting her knee into my stomach, making it clear she was taking my car. Grabbing me by the neck, she pulled me down the hall and threw me into a disgusting hole of a room.

Even in the dark it was obvious someone lived in the room and was gone at the moment. There was an unmade single bed, and a mangy nightstand topped with an old-fashioned lamp muted by the towel covering its shade. Along the bleak wall, a beat-up old dresser missing most of its knobs filled the empty space. As I frantically looked around, I heard her lock the bedroom door – from the outside. Terrified, I knew my life was radically different than it had been just one hour earlier. Frightened to make any movements or sound, I quietly adjusted the curtains on the long horizontal window to shed moonlight into the room in which I was now a prisoner. The view was of a small backyard with rusted patio furniture, overgrown shrubs infested by weeds, and a porch without screens. I searched hysterically for the face of a neighbor; there was no one to help me in this direction. I tried to open the window to escape, but it was either painted or nailed shut.

I looked around the room. Dirty clothes were thrown on the floor, along with old food wrappers, which smelled like bitter fruit. The green carpet was worn and dirty. I frantically looked for family photographs or some semblance of normalcy inside this hell. Nothing told me of what was to come, or whose room I now occupied uninvited. I quietly sat on the floor, knees to chest, head down, leaning against the bed praying for God to spare me harm, and take me home. I begged forgiveness as I promised to get help and never return to this neighborhood. I felt a moment of relief, but help never came. I silently stood up and walked in circles around the room, trying to soothe the fretfulness piercing my soul. As I gained confidence, a new anxiety reared its ugly head: what if someone was hiding behind the closed closet doors waiting to ambush me on my next circuit around the room? I took a deep breath, expecting the worse, and threw open the old shutter style doors. Relieved of paranoia when no one was inside, I curiously looked through the wardrobe, finding ragged flannel shirts, jeans, and various hip hop t-shirts in multiple colors. The wardrobe was as scarce as the furnishing inside the room. Sitting back down on the ragged carpet, I remembered that Tina wanted my car. For sure, this would be another escapade with my car.

Before Tina took off, she barged into the bedroom, dragged me out, and made me sign a makeshift contract stating I allowed her to use my car. Tina gave strict instructions to the others in the room to prevent me from leaving or making any contact with my family. She snatched up my keys before locking us all inside the house.

There were four of us. Thomas, a mahogany-colored man in his fifties who looked damaged from years of addiction and the hard work needed to support his habit. Surprisingly, he was a gentle man, soft-spoken with a lean body and a simple smile. His wife, Linda, a white woman in her late forties, was weirdly out of place in this house. She, too, was unusually soft-spoken, but she seemed balanced and happy to live in such squalor. Jackson, in his late twenties, must have been a remarkable little boy. In spite of being locked in a crack house, he was polite and had a confident demeanor. Little did I know that each of these three strangers would one day be remembered as heroes. I wondered; how did they get into this dark, drug-induced, roach-infested predicament? Perhaps the same way I did -- one hit at a time.

For the next four days I was held prisoner – locked inside this house with these strangers and kept alone in the bedroom much of the time while Tina used my Grand Am to make her drug runs. I wasn't allowed to leave the room other than to use the restroom or get a glass of water. Starving without food, a woman assigned to watch over me gave me a piece of her fried chicken. I ate with determination because I didn't know if I would ever eat again. Crying out loud, I begged and begged for someone to let me go home. I wanted my cell phone back. I wanted so badly to get word to my parents or my brother that I was alive. For hours, I sat imagining the grief and sorrow my family was feeling since my disappearance. I would daydream about what I would say to my mom and dad if I ever got to see them again. I would kneel against the bed praying for God to save me.

Sitting in my "prison cell" of a bedroom, I was on a crazy drug trip. Tina would pull up in my car, drop off a handful of drugs, and I would stay continually stoned. Yet even though I was high and paranoid, I tried to focus on the fact that I had guardian angels protecting me. I prayed to God for help, and tried to thank him for keeping me alive long enough to turn 30 years old.

Word got around that I was in the drug house. My regular drug dealer, Eric, had a cousin named Rodney to whom I owed $50. When Rodney learned I was at Tina's place, he came over and began pounding on the front door. I couldn't open it because I had been locked in from the outside.

"You're in my neighborhood now, bitch!" he screamed, adding plenty of vulgar and colorful words. "I want my fifty bucks you white, snobby bitch. You'd better find a way to get me my money or I will kill your fucking ass."

Petrified, I answered through the door, "As soon as Tina lets me out of this house, I'll find my bank card and get you the money."

Rodney tried to kick the front door in but was unsuccessful. That only enraged him more. He wanted his money and decided to rile up the neighborhood. At this point, the three strangers transferred me from the room facing the back of the house to Thomas's room near the front of the house. His room was bare, with old terrazzo floors that stayed cool to the touch. There was a simply decorated queen-sized bed he shared with Linda, and a cheap abstract framed picture from the Seventies above it. They had a small white refrigerator along a wall, with two chairs and a table supporting a toaster and coffee maker. There was a wooden ledge they used for storing groceries and personal hygiene products. A television perched on another bookshelf with other knickknacks. Their closet was full of clothes, scrap books, and a stack of old record albums almost five feet tall. I could tell this small room inside the crack house was their private world. Somehow, they had made this awful place a "home." Linda was inside the room, propped up on her bed smoking dope and watching television, when Thomas and Jackson hurried me across the hall and inside this new hideout.

A huge crowd grew outside the window, getting louder and louder. "I'll shoot her upside the head," I heard Rodney boast. Faceless men standing outside the window began to make threats against my life. I heard fierce voices threatening to rape me. They would laugh and describe how they would prove that a rich white girl couldn't come into their neighborhood, steal from a black man, and get away with it. As others joined the group outside, and I heard them plan how they would to kill me, I began to sob uncontrollably. I knew that I was in grave danger; I had crossed into a world of street politics I didn't understand and could not control. The mob of men cheered and began banging on the window, trying to break it. They moved from window to window trying to find out where I was hiding. They came to the front door, hammering and beating on it to gain entrance into the house, where room by room they planned to hunt me down. These were gang members and criminals ready to back up their boy, wronged by this rich white chick.

I knew I had little time before someone would get his hands on me. I cowered in the closet, hiding behind the stacked records, praying and trying to make a deal with God. My blood pressure soared as I envisioned a dozen men breaking down the bedroom door, pulling me out of the closet, raping and beating me until I was totally broken. Then, once I was totally violated, they would kill me. I visualized my mom and dad crying over the loss of their once-beautiful daughter. I was heartbroken, horrified, and completely terrified as I heard my name chanted outside the feeble walls. Through the windows, they would say, "Mary Jane, we are coming in. Mary Jane, we are coming to find you." One guy kept making comments about wanting to rape me so he could prove I was wrong for not paying Rodney back.

Thomas must have grown tired of the escalating riot, because he ran outside and tried to calm everyone. It didn't work. Through the window I heard a huge fight break out. The sudden sounds reminded me of a lion pride fighting over the recent kill. Roars of anger came from some men with louder voices who shouted obscene words while others banged on the window with pieces of rebar. I heard others, who perhaps were the weaker members, fighting off to the side of the house. I have no idea what happened exactly but it must have been terrible. Moments later, miraculously, Thomas managed to get back inside the house, slammed the door, and stumbled through the bedroom doorway. Frozen in horror, I could see his arm was broken in multiple places. His face was beaten with one eye completely shut; his lip was split wide open and bleeding, and his mutilated arm swung off uselessly to his right side. Thomas couldn't control his sobbing due to the pain of his numerous injuries, and he was headed to the hospital. "Mary Jane, I can't help you anymore," he groaned. "You're on your own. Stay in the closet and don't come out until someone comes to get you." I felt crazed with anger for what they had done to him. Yet, I was powerless and still in severe danger.

Tina suddenly pulled up in the driveway, in my car. She rushed into the house and began planning the escape to take Thomas to the hospital. Frantically, I pleaded with Tina, "Please don't leave me here alone. I promise to stay low in the backseat. Just drop me off somewhere and I promise not to tell anyone. Please take me with you to the hospital. If you leave me here, they will kill me." Tina shrugged me off, demanding I stay behind. She assigned the woman who walked into the house with her to stay behind with me. As I perched to look outside the window, I watched Tina pay Rodney the $50. I heard her shouting at the men outside that if anyone so much as put one finger on me, they'd have a huge debt to pay. Tina's brother was a major drug kingpin in that neighborhood, who -- even from jail -- had the power to maim or kill anyone who disobeyed his commands. As Tina pulled away with Thomas in my car, the noise and the threats on my life began again. This time, the mob was louder and more destructive, breaking glass, banging iron rods against one another, and destroying the outside patio furniture. The front door became a pounding drum; they were trying to beat the door down.

I cowered behind any junk I could find in the closet, envisioning the local news report that there had been a brutal gang rape and murder of one of the "twenty most eligible bachelorettes" in Orlando. I saw the funeral procession, the hearse, and tears on the faces of my family. I begged God to keep me from dying this way. I wanted to make things right with my mom. My heart was beating so fast that I prayed I would die of a heart attack rather than what I knew was coming. I imagined a beating first, followed by rape, and finally death. I succumbed to my own fatality.

Jackson, the young black man from across the hall, walked in the room, grabbed my hand, and lifted me out of the closet. He said, "Lady, calm down or you will have a heart attack and die. You've got to breathe. You are in serious trouble, but you have got to keep your head about you right now."

Strangely, we sat on the edge of the bed and he held my hands to comfort me, careful not to move or speak so that no one outside would hear us and know what room I was in. Once I caught my breath, the woman Tina assigned to watch over me came in, grabbed my wrist, and took me to the original bedroom – Tina's room – where this nightmare began. The thumping on the windows continued for hours while the violent men lingered outside. My large female "bodyguard" offered me a few hits to keep me prisoner in mind and body. I gladly accepted because I wanted so badly to escape. The sounds moved from the front of the house to the side where I was hiding. I ached with sadness. As I heard voices move near the window, I slid behind the eight-foot armoire in Tina's room, and hunched in the corner so no one could see me through the blinds. Terrified, I stayed there and the so-called bodyguard eventually left me there to fend for myself. I remained in the corner, in tears and dog-tired from the hours of off-and-on window banging. Hours later, Thomas and Linda returned from the hospital. I demanded to know, "Where is Tina? Why is she leaving me here to die?" Neither Thomas nor Linda replied. My guess is that Tina bribed them in some way to stay silent about me, the fighting, his injuries, and Tina's whereabouts.

Now in the wee hours of the morning, the noise outside ceased and I begged Thomas to allow me to sleep on their cold, damp floor. I promised not to move, speak, or cause any trouble. They must have known I was still in unbelievable danger. By the grace of God, they showed me kindness by giving me a thin blanket, a tiny white pillow, and a small space at the foot of their queen-sized bed. Lights were out, and I could hear Thomas groaning in pain. My heart broke as I lay there helpless. I didn't dare fall asleep for fear someone would break down the bedroom door. It grew eerily quiet and I lay still, watching the dim lights in the gap under the door. Occasionally, I saw footsteps move along the hallway. No words were spoken. Paralyzed in fear, I'd watch for them to move past the door. I didn't dare breathe as they walked by. Though I will never know who walked through the house later that night, my guess is that it was Jackson and the bodyguard checking on the status inside the house. The Devil himself loves chaos and harm. I truly believe the battle for my life was more spiritual than physical. I believe the reason the gang outside didn't break in was because my guardian angel, the warrior, stood guard. Threatening to take my life over 50 bucks isn't rational; though the fighting manifested in the physical realm, it started in the minds of evil men who had lost contact with God.

The next morning was my thirtieth birthday. As I sat up, I realized the riot outside was over. I was in complete shambles, emotionally. I hadn't eaten anything substantive or slept in four days.

Thomas had been my only defender so I tried to sweet-talk him into letting me go. I offered to send him money once I returned home. I told him it was my birthday and my parents would be looking for me. "Until Tina comes back, you don't leave," he said. I'm sure he was angry that his act of goodwill had gotten him nothing but a broken arm, a black eye, multiple stitches above his upper lip, and an unwanted house guest.

Finally, later that morning, Jackson came home with news that Tina had been busted for selling drugs. There was no reason to keep me anymore. He warned Thomas, "You better get her out of here because Tina's in jail and they've impounded the white girl's car. The police are driving around the streets now looking for her."

The house full of men I had never seen before arrived shortly after Jackson, and they didn't know what to do with me. If they let me walk out of the house, there was a chance a patrol car would round the corner and I'd be seen walking out of the place. A blond-haired, green-eyed Caucasian woman would draw the wrong kind of attention to the crack house. At the same time, no one wanted to stow me away in their vehicle for fear of being caught kidnapping. The men decided the latter was a better option but warned me not to sit up in the back seat of the car. Within minutes, a tall thin stranger, who had never met me before, hurriedly stowed me in his back seat and drove slowly down the street while listening to rap music. I began to fear that he might be taking me to a vague location to "finish me off" since I knew information about Tina, the drug deals inside the crack house, and the names of those who came and went over the four days I was held prisoner. I was relieved when he dropped me off at a neighborhood gas station.

Two minutes later, a patrol car pulled up and the officer said they had been looking for me. I broke down and sobbed while calling my dad from the officer's phone. The policeman took a look at my driver's license and said, "You are beautiful in this picture."

"Thanks," I muttered.

"You're in over your head, young lady. I've worked this neighborhood for years and you won't resemble this picture in a year if you keep coming back."

My dad drove up in his brown Mercedes and we collapsed in each other's arms. I cried, repeating over and over, "I don't want to do this. I don't want to be here anymore."

He remembers:

When I picked her up she said she was done. She looked like hell. To this day, I still don't know what went on those four days she was kidnapped. I don't know if I want to ever know.

My mom:

I think I was with my mother that afternoon. Joe didn't want me in the car with Mary Jane. He didn't want me to see her like that, in that neighborhood. I went to my mom's to hide out and protect myself.

Dad took me to the hospital but they wouldn't admit me. Detoxing from crack is more of a physical breakdown than detoxification from alcohol. Mom got on the phone and agreed to look for a treatment facility. She found a place called Alternatives in Treatments, three hours away in West Palm Beach.

My mom eventually arrived and she ran to the car to see me through the window. Aghast, she backed away. By now, my eyes were barely open from hunger, fatigue, and post-traumatic stress. Both my mom and I silently agreed we didn't have the strength in that moment to embrace one another. We were both hardly able to conceive our reality. Without a word, she placed her hand on the glass of the passenger's window, began to cry, and stepped back from me. I, too, began to weep inside the car, grateful to be alive. Mom met Dad in the parking lot of the hospital and they talked about me as if I wasn't there. I wasn't allowed to speak as I sat in the back seat. It was like I was a child all over again – and I was. My life choices had gotten me to the point where I was incapable of taking care of myself. I needed my parents to make the decisions for me.

"I cannot handle her," my mother said. "This is too dangerous. She needs to be some place where someone professional can help her."

She picks up the story later in my transition to the treatment center:

Mary Jane was out cold, just done. Passed out. She had barely survived being kidnapped and was lucky to be alive. I sat in the back seat with her head in my lap on the way to West Palm Beach. She slept from the time we packed her bags to the moment we arrived.

I remember the snapshot they took of her at the treatment center. Her hair was pulled straight back and it was filthy dirty. Her skin was gray and looked old and haggard. Leaving her there was the toughest thing we had ever done.

When it was time to write the check, we found out the bill came to nearly the same amount Joe and I had received in the mail that day. Praise God!

My dad continues:

We didn't have extra money because we had just opened a business and were struggling. I had just received a check that day for a house closing for thirty-six hundred dollars and had just deposited it.

The first payment for Mary Jane's treatment was thirty-three hundred dollars. I told Leigh, "God works in mysterious ways." The fact that he had provided was like divine-guided intercession. He knew we needed that money to get our girl where she needed to be.

Being checked into the rehab center on my thirtieth birthday was heart-wrenching for me. We arrived at the treatment center around 10:00 p.m. I felt completely wiped out and I could barely stand. I vaguely remember getting out of the car, grabbing my purse in search of makeup to cover up the emotional scars of my last four days. Furious, my dad yelled, "What in the hell are you doing Mary Jane? No amount of makeup will cover your mistakes!" He was correct. I didn't know what city I was in or where they had taken me. I thought, *will I ever go home again?* I walked into what appeared to be the check-in area, where they took my photograph, my blood pressure, and asked us basic questions. Molly and Dove checked me in that night. I will always remember them for their kindness.

My parents and I embraced one last time, as though saying goodbye forever. It was incredibly hard to watch them leave the facility, not knowing when I would see them. They had been my lifeline and my prayer warriors for several years. As my parents left me behind, I walked into a room full of addicts who welcomed me to the facility. I remember all sorts of men and women sitting on a couch inside the main television area, laughing as they watched a movie. I felt as though I was in a time warp. Only 12 hours earlier, I had been in a life-threatening situation surrounded by violence, drug dealers, and prostitutes, and I couldn't comprehend what was happening. Who were these smiling faces? I hadn't laughed or smiled in a long time. What impact would they have in my life? Where did they come from? Where was I that so many people gathered together?

Moments later, I was escorted to a bedroom just off to the right of the manager's office where I changed into pajamas. Only a dim light lit the room, and there were two neatly made twin beds that lined the wall. Though I didn't know where I was, I knew I was finally safe and in good hands. I slept for two days, interrupted only when the patient techs checked to see if I was breathing. Though I had major bruises on my legs and arms from being pulled around and shoved into different rooms, my physical injuries were minor. The lump on the back of my head from Tina shoving me into the wall had since disappeared. The patient techs would take my temperature, and to prevent dehydration they would ask me to sit up to drink water throughout my 48 hours of sleeping. On the third day, a tall lean woman named Doreen nudged me until I was coherent. She gave me orders to get up, eat, and get ready to attend a meeting. I stumbled around the dim room, trying to acclimate to my surroundings. Still unaware of exactly where I was, I put on my blue jeans, a yellow tank top, and flip flops. At their house, my mom and I had packed a bag with my favorite clothes and shoes before we left Orlando.

Others were eating in the common area, but I was unable to keep anything down. We loaded into a big white van and traveled to a meeting hall. As I sat outside of the Recovery clubhouse, a woman named Shannon came to me, smiled, and shook my hand. She was the first normal-looking person I had seen in months.

CHAPTER FIFTEEN

Inside the rehab center I received a letter from my mom. It read:

~

Dearest Mary Jane,

Remember when no one else believed you could compete on the swim team because of your serious ear problems? You found a way to not just be on the team but to be number one. Remember when you wanted to be a cheerleader but hundreds of girls tried out for the few spots? You found a way to win your spot and earn All American Cheerleader, too.

Remember when your grades said "junior college" but your heart said "university?" You found a way to go to UCF as a cheerleader, join Zeta, Little Sister, O-Team, and on and on and on all the way to graduation day.

Mary Jane, there is great power in making a commitment to bettering your life. You have proven that in so many ways and on so many days.

You will find your way now because you never give up, you never give in, and you never walk alone. I believe in you!

Love,
Mom XO

~

I, in turn, began to journal my own thoughts:

I can't seem to "get it together" on my own. My health isn't very good and I'm afraid if I don't take care of this soon, my body would eventually give up the fight. I'm sure I've only made it this far because I'm stubborn.

Tonight I sit outside for the first time in months, appreciating the night air and smell of the trees and the surroundings. However, I feel very depressed and alone. My mind tells me I should just give up and continue on the journey to the bottom. But the few memories I have tell me to run toward the light of the Lord and hold on.

How come a drug high is more gratifying than a sale I made for my company worth $3 million? When did I decide that a night out with my friends partying would be more worthwhile than time with a significant other or my family? When did I begin choosing pain over joy?

I keep flashing back to winning Homecoming Queen for Lake Charles High School. I remember my brother getting the entire freshman football team to chant my name when I went by. Driving by the stadium full of screaming friends, family members, and acquaintances, I remember how afraid I was that someone in the crowd would be jealous of me for winning. Rather than feeling happy and fortunate that thousands of people were showing me love, I was focused on the one or two people out there who didn't want me to win. Where did I learn all that shame, guilt, and fear?

Allison, my best friend, once told me I was really hard to get close to. I was shocked! She and I shared everything, so I thought, but really, she had shared and I had listened. When I was hurting or suffering, I simply hid my emotions by smiling and pretending I was okay.

Now I'm at the point where hiding doesn't work. I'm not that good an actress. My face and eyes show that I am not a happy young woman. I'm afraid to run into anyone I know. I'm tired of putting on a happy face and telling people I'm great. Mom always said, "Eighty percent of people don't care you're having a bad day. And the other twenty percent are glad." That's one hundred percent of the people, right? So who really cares about my bad day, anyway?

I want to believe most people care, within the limits of their time constraints. I figure most people just want to hear a polite answer – not the real story. The real story of my life would cut into their daily schedule. I have become accustomed to providing shallow answers that don't reveal too much about my personal life. I've been taught by my parents, teachers, and role models that people don't like people who don't have it all together. In order to have lots of friends and respect from your peers, people learn to hide their shortcomings and only share the 'good' things in life.

I think the only way to have true friends is to be myself. I need to allow myself to be vulnerable and tell the ones I love that I am hurting.

After two months of rehab, I did meet someone who would become a "true friend" for the rest of my life. I stood in church on a Wednesday night and sang the praise choruses up on the overhead screens. There was a woman standing on stage in the worship team who kept glancing at me, and we continued making eye contact until the end of the song.

When the pastor invited everyone in the auditorium to walk around and introduce themselves, I thought to myself, *I'm gonna go shake that woman's hand.* I headed to the base of the stage and extended my arm.

"I'm Mary Jane."

"Kerrie, nice to meet you."

I had been praying for female friends. I was lonely and my heart yearned for a sister in Christ who had what I wanted and could bring out the best in me.

Kerrie's take:

From the stage view, I could see her sitting in the audience. I'd never seen her before but I thought, "Gosh, she just looks like a sunflower." She had long, curly, blonde hair and I thought to myself that I'd really like to get to know her. When it was time to shake hands, she walked down to the stage and shook mine. I thought that was unusual. Generally people in the crowd didn't approach the platform.

From there we started connecting. We went to a women's luncheon and became friends. I just thought she was very confident and outgoing. I was divorced and single and the two of us were in the same boat. I had faced problems in life and was attending recovery meetings for alcohol addiction, but it took a while for Mary Jane to open up about her drug problems.

One of the things I noticed was that she was very guarded. I wondered why she didn't trust me. She was often very elusive and cold at times, and I couldn't understand why. I thought she didn't like me or that I wasn't cool enough for her.

She and I attended meetings together but I never really knew what the truth was with Mary Jane. I liked her but she was a tough person to figure out.

CHAPTER SIXTEEN

After hiding away in the rehab center for 45 days, my counselor declared my addiction treatment complete and encouraged me to venture back out in public. On Halloween, my first holiday sober in many, many years, I tried to find a safe activity and decided to attend a bowl-a-thon with some friends from recovery. It felt like my first big night of freedom after the rigor and routine of the rehab.

A handsome bodybuilder bowling in the lane next to us distracted me from my game. We were introduced through a mutual acquaintance. His name was Steven, and our conversation intensified. When he mentioned something about Christ, suddenly he was even more attractive to me -- a hot, sober man of Christ. I thought God was finally giving me a break in the romance department.

In treatment I began to reconnect with Jesus, starting with the simple act of kneeling at the end of my bed. With the sun shining through the window and on my face, I would ask every morning, as earnestly as I could muster, for God to fill every fiber, every cell, every muscle of my body with recovery. I begged forgiveness for my sins and shared with Him a desire to change.

Steven had also been through treatment and was eight years sober, which is why he should have known better than to "13th-Step" me. There are 12 Steps of recovery, and when you 13th-Step someone, it means you try to date them. It is strongly suggested not to date someone in the first year of recovery. Because I was still a wreck at that moment, I should have heeded this advice.

I was so vulnerable and broken then — still dealing with post-traumatic stress in the aftermath of being held prisoner and threatened with rape and death for four days, along with all the hurtful memories of loss and pain I caused others. So before long, I found myself being brainwashed by this magnetic Jesus-fanatic. I thought Steven was "the one." I began attending his church and meeting his friends. I believed that his world was my ticket out of the hell I had created in my own life.

After only four months of dating, Steven asked me to marry him and I said no. "I can't marry you. I'm new in recovery," I argued.

"Everybody else says you can't," he said. "But we're special and different."

I wasn't sure about that, but I did like the stability that marriage offered. I should have been more suspicious when Steven suggested we hide our engagement from my parents. Whenever someone suggests you lie and keep secrets from the ones you love, you should see that as a clue that things are amiss. Even though I usually told my family everything, I agreed to go along with Steven's secrecy plan. I struggled with this deep inside, yet due to so many other overriding emotions that demanded immediate attention through meetings and therapy, I became a pushover for love. I also became a pushover for his ideals: That I become a personal trainer and follow in his career path.

I was 30 years old when we got married on the beach, with *his* pastor officiating and *his* two friends as witnesses. No one from my life was present. I didn't buy a dress; I wore expensive white Capri pants and a lavender tank top. The morning of my wedding I drove to a floral shop, where Joseph, the owner of the store, made me a beautiful bouquet of mixed fresh flowers exploding with color and aroma.

Hours before the simple ceremony, I asked Steven to reconsider. I begged him to postpone the wedding until we were ready to share the news with my family. Smugly, he disagreed and we moved forward. However, that day I felt empty without my family and knew I wasn't doing the right thing for myself. My soul knew this was another catastrophic mistake. Yet, I was still a prisoner of my own failures, weak and desperate for love. So, despite the lies and the lavender tank top, I still said "I do."

I have to admit we were a beautiful couple. Steven and I worked out and dieted all the time. We went to meetings together and he was all the things I thought I wanted to have and to hold.

For a few months, I did very well with sobriety. I was personal training high-end clients and I *looked* very healthy. I had 11% body fat and I was "shredded," as they say, with ripped triceps, muscular chest striations, and overall muscle tone. We opened our own business, a personal training studio and health food store, but Steven was the primary owner. By superficial appearances, I had my act together with brief moments of serenity and joy.

On Easter, I took a good friend and her new baby daughter to my family's house for dinner. Steven was supposed to join us. We were going to tell my parents that he and I were "engaged," just to ease them gently into the news of our marriage. But Steven never showed up that day to make the announcement, with no good reason. This was his devious way of controlling me and the marriage, and a few months later, I relapsed on crack, prescription drugs like Xanax, Valium, and Vicodin, and alcohol.

Kerrie remembers that time frame better than I do:

George, a friend from recovery, told me Mary Jane was in a bad way. He said I needed to get in touch with her. I called and she didn't answer or return my call. She had disappeared on a drug binge.

I wanted to be supportive but knew if the person wasn't ready, it wasn't going to happen.

Finally, she returned my call. I told her I needed to talk. We had become very good friends and we had shared a lot about our lives together.

She came to my house and sat across from me on the couch, staring at me like she was so ticked off to even be there. Her look was like, "How dare you even call me to come over to your house to talk to you?"

It was so nerve-wracking for me to have that conversation. I said, "Mary Jane, I cannot watch you continue to do what you're doing and not say anything or call you on it. You're on the fence when it comes to getting clean and you need to make a decision -- either have both feet in the program and do the work or you're not going to make it." She knew what that meant. She was going to die.

She didn't say anything to me. She just looked at me with a blank stare, as cold as ice. I told her she could either accept this and our friendship would continue to grow or I would never see her again. I wasn't giving her an ultimatum. I just knew she would start blocking me out of her life.

I took Kerrie's words to heart and went into an all-women's treatment facility to get clean again. Steven visited me there during a group session. In front of the entire room of recovering addicts, he said that he had taken it upon himself to tell my parents we were married.

"Are you kidding me?" I snapped.

I called my folks and sure enough, our marriage was no longer a secret. They seemed surprised and disappointed that I hadn't told them, but they were smart enough to see who Steven really was. They could see a manipulator from a mile off.

My therapists were worried about me. They said I should never have married him during such a vulnerable time in my recovery. They suggested I avoid even returning to the apartment we shared, once I had completed treatment.

"You are in grave danger," one of them said. "This guy is controlling... you need time to heal. You're gonna outgrow him one day. You've just got the wrong guy." In my mind, I wasn't sure they were telling me the truth. I still loved Steven, or thought I did.

My parents came to visit me in treatment, and although my brother couldn't face me there, his heartfelt letter arrived a few days afterward:

~

Mary Jane,

Hello and God bless! You've probably spent the day with Mom and Dad and I hope you had a great visit. I'm sorry I couldn't make it, but if it's okay with you, I'd like to come down next Sunday and visit you.

I'm sending you this picture so you can remember what I look like and how much I love you! I want to tell you that I respect you for your decision to receive more counseling and your courage to stay sober. I hate that the Devil tries day in and out to weaken our bond with God. You are very special and I hope that before my life is over and I go to visit the Good Lord, I will be half the person you are. Don't get down on yourself or worry how other people feel or think. You are Mary Jane Smith and the only thing you have to answer to is yourself and God.

"I was hungry and you gave me something to eat, I was thirsty and you gave me something to drink. I needed clothes and you clothed me. I was sick and you looked after me." Matthew 25:35-36

The Lord Jesus Christ loves you, good and bad. He forgives us no matter what. Of course the decisions we've made affect our future. But the beautiful thing about life is that tomorrow is a new day, a new start, and best of all -- we can make a choice.

I know you may be feeling lonely or sad or mad but remember – I pray for you every day. I know that Mary Jane will beat Satan and will be my sister for a long time to come. Remember to keep the faith, pray every day, and when you look in the mirror say, "I'm sober, drug free, and proud to be me!" (I just made that up.)

I love you so much. Stay strong. Call me collect if you get a chance. I love, respect, miss, and look up to you very much!

Your Loving Brother,
Chad

∾

After four weeks of treatment, I got out. And yes, I did drugs again shortly after going home. I was in over my head with this marriage and wasn't prepared for this chapter of my life. I was still traumatized and spiritually ill from the months of chaos, upheaval, and perpetuating Steven's lies. I was officially diagnosed with post-traumatic stress disorder, which explained why I was acting out. Steven's overbearing and controlling behavior tipped me into temptation, and I just wasn't strong enough yet to stand up for myself.

On a high, I barricaded myself inside our apartment. When Steven came home, I tried to lock him out. We weren't getting along and he was staying with friends for days at a time. I'm sure I didn't want him to see me high. "It's late. Come back tomorrow," I shouted through the door.

But he put his key in the lock, forcing the door open with all 240 pounds, and charged through. He pushed me out of the way, and I pushed him back. Then he shoved me against the wall. I got scared, threw a water glass at him, and left the house the first chance I got.

Steven called the police and told them I had "battered" him. This was such a lie on his part; clearly, what we did wasn't right but neither one of us really did any "battering." We had pushed each other, the way you'd shove someone out of the way. We were both angry, yet neither of us were hurt or participated in rough treatment.

But when I returned to my apartment from a trip to buy more drugs, I found law enforcement waiting for me. They told me I was being arrested for domestic battery and took me to jail for the night.

It was incredibly humiliating that they believed Steven over me. I said, "You don't understand. He pushed me first and I pushed him back. That was the whole altercation. Look at the two of us. I'm one hundred pounds and he's two hundred forty, all muscle. How could I domestically hurt him?"

Steven put on a good act for the police -- and it didn't help that they some of my drug paraphernalia under the guestroom bed when searching the house. From a law enforcement perspective, he was the clean and sober citizen; I was the addict. I was devastated and inconsolable, and wished I was dead. My heart broke that night in jail. I felt abandoned by Steven. I knew he lied to the officers intentionally to hurt and enrage me. I was wrong to use drugs, but for Steven to lie to the police about domestic abuse was one of the most painful experiences of my life because it was totally against my belief system. I would never strike anyone. While in jail that night, I dreamed of revenge, starting with slashing the tires on his stupid truck. I loathed him, the marriage vows we took, my life, and I despised my defenselessness.

Once out of jail, I quickly moved out of our apartment, moved in with acquaintances, and moved on with my new life. I promised myself that I would never give my heart away again, and that I would protect my mind from men who use women to get their way. When I saw him at future meetings, I wanted to walk up to him and scream, "You have ruined my life you lousy, selfish bastard."

As a result of the charge, I agreed to 12 weeks of out-patient abuse counseling. During that time, the counselor studied the files and realized it was actually me who was abused verbally and mentally. They discovered that Steven had a criminal history prior to our relationship. Inside our demented rapport he was manipulative, and verbally and emotionally abusive.

The counseling was valuable and taught me to empower myself, to see the big picture. I probably got the help I needed. I was living in a halfway house, and that's where I was served divorce papers.

Heartsick over how I had allowed my life to spin out of control and married the wrong man, I sobbed hysterically, clutching the thick envelope to my chest. Reflecting back, I asked myself and God, "How did I get here?" It was a long night of tears. I was in a strange, uncomfortable environment and felt the sting of a failed marriage. However, I connected with the Lord that night as I lay crying and meditating on my bed. Suddenly, without warning, I envisioned myself inside a white cloud and the Holy Spirit whispered, *"This is my beloved Son, in whom I am well pleased. Hear Him!"* I didn't know the significance of the white cloud or the words I heard in the moment. I sat up, went over to my Bible, picked it up, and opened the book directly to Matthew 17:5-8. Remarkably, there was a white cloud described in the verses, just like the one I envisioned surrounding me during my meditation. In this passage, Jesus came to the suffering disciples, touched them, and said, "Arise, and do not be afraid." It was a scripture that I came to lean on during this time. Those passages renewed my inner strength to move forward whenever I became worried and concerned.

Kerrie took pity on me and welcomed me into her home.

Her words:

When she called me and told me she had no place to go or to live, I told her to come on over. She stayed in my daughter's room and lived with me for six months. I was a little more naïve than I am now.

Mary Jane brought an addict into my home when I wasn't there and months later, after she moved out, I believe he came back and stole a bunch of things from my daughter's room, jewelry and stuff like that. It was upsetting to me because those were my daughter's things. I don't blame her because I cannot be sure it was him. Mary Jane also racked up my phone bill to $350. That was a big hit for me at the time. I didn't have a lot of money but I never brought it up to her.

She frequently stood me up for planned events. I learned to always have a back-up plan because I couldn't depend on Mary Jane to keep her word. She was very secretive and didn't tell me a lot, still pretending to be someone else in front of me. I knew she was lost and hurting. There were a couple times she came into my bedroom in the middle of the night and said, "I'm scared. Can I sleep with you?" I said, "Yeah, get in bed." She was afraid of the dark, of the unknown. I still didn't know the whole story yet. I didn't fully understand her fears. It wasn't until a couple years later that she started divulging her past. Once she began telling me the stories of her past, then I understood why she was so timid and afraid.

Throughout all the chaos, we still had a bond. I knew she was sick and I didn't want to harbor animosity. I just loved her and continued to pray for her healing.

As I look back on my failed marriage to Steven, I no longer resent or blame him for my mistakes and decisions. I believe that like me, he did the best he could at that time. He was also healing from life experiences when we met. I have realized I am solely responsible for my own actions. My drug use was the ultimate reason I suffered so much in that relationship. Sober-minded women choose better mates.

CHAPTER SEVENTEEN

I was a crack addict who could never stay in one place for long, running from one apartment to the next. After leaving Kerrie's home, I found roommates, one male and one female. Gunther and Charlene fought all the time and smoked incessantly. Yet, they were also responsible for helping a lot of recovering alcoholics and addicts by providing a meal or giving them a ride to a meeting. Charlene was a strong-willed woman who got sober young and was determined to stay clean. She and Gunther were my saving grace on many days when I desperately needed a safe place to stay and a word of encouragement. I lived in their small cottage for several months. They opened their home to me; shared their experience, strength and hope, and for that I will be forever grateful.

After that lease expired, I journeyed even further into an emotional abyss. Kerrie visited me while I was living in a tiny hole-in-the-wall hovel at the end of a dirt road. I loved that place; though it was small, it had character. I planted a small garden out front alongside a simple pebbled porch where I would sit and listen to music. It was one of the gifts I left behind. I had received a big settlement from a car accident, which paid the rent and all my expenses -- including alcohol and drugs -- for six months. Now, I had enough money to kill myself.

Kerrie wasn't sure whether I was going to make it out of that little shack alive. Luckily, years before I adopted a great big Rottweiler named Pugsley, and she was my salvation. I finally found a friend who didn't know the difference between sobriety and addiction. This dog was my lifeline and I loved her dearly. We did everything together since I was scarcely working. She watched over me, my furry guardian angel.

Pugs and I ate breakfast, lunch, and dinner together. It was almost certain I would get fresh air daily because she demanded a walk alongside the train tracks where she could run free. I would follow and watch her dash wildly through the fields. This was the only moment of joy I had every day. She loved me no matter what and I needed that love – even if it came from a dog -- to stay grounded.

One afternoon as I showered, my heart began to beat very fast, either from fatigue and lack of good food, or strain from all the late nights. Frightened, I stepped out of the water to call for help. As I leaned down and wrapped myself in a towel, Pugs moved in close to me, pushed me to the floor, and laid on my lap to warm me up. She leaned in closely, intuiting I was in some kind of danger. I believe her warmth settled my nerves and prevented me from passing out. That day, she didn't leave my side. Though she seemed upset with me, Pugsley just sat close and watched me. That evening when I got into bed, she hopped up alongside me, lying close as if to guard me. As I drifted off to sleep, I caught her watching me. I will always be grateful for her unconditional love and patience.

One night, I stayed at my friend James's house. He had gone off to work and I was partying by myself. Around midnight, I called my mom and we talked for an hour.

Still trying to mend our fractured relationship, I opened up to her. I sat on James's bed with a late-night TV show in the background, attempting to explain what it was like to be so far away in my mind, so addicted to this substance.

"You can do it, Mary Jane," she urged. "I understand that it's hard and that you're really fighting." She knew I had gotten myself into something I could not control and was battling for my life. I wanted her to know that even though I was becoming "that" person, I still loved her.

My mom explains:

We did anything and everything to keep her off the streets, believing it was going to turn around for her. We came down at one point and rented her a cute apartment, filled it with new furniture from Rooms-To-Go, and a week later we couldn't find her. I was forever trying to figure out why I couldn't buy my daughter out of her troubles!

She would call us from somewhere and say she wanted to meet us there. We would drive from Orlando to West Palm Beach only to find her gone from the meeting location. Unable to reach her, sometimes we stayed in West Palm Beach for two or three days and waited for Mary Jane to reemerge from her hiding spot. Eventually, we gave up and drove home.

I hurt my parents over and over. One Mother's Day weekend, I promised my mom I would come home to Orlando and go out to breakfast at her favorite beachfront restaurant. But I never showed up for her special day. I was with a drug buddy. At 3:00 p.m., I finally worked up the courage to call her and thought for sure she was just going to let me have it.

I'll never forget her words: "My Mary Jane would never miss Mother's Day." She quietly asked me to pack up and come home. Again, she knew that the sober Mary Jane underneath all this anguish would never miss a holiday with her.

This offering of grace stayed with me forever. In that moment, she created more hope for me, and gave me yet another gift of unconditional love.

The cute little studio apartment, which I also describe as "my hovel," lasted a few more months while I tried to get my life back by working as a waitress at T.G.I. Friday's. It was a far cry from my career as a highly paid sales executive, but I was grateful to have a job as I slowly started my re-entry into the world.

Two plus years came and went. I would have incredible year-long periods of sobriety, but then I would crash. I had one foot in the world of recovery and wellness, and one foot in the underground world of drugs, thugs, and alcoholic behavior. I had new friends with fantastic relationships, strong ties in the work community, and respectable lives of service in church and recovery. I tagged along. I met and closely followed a small group of Christian recovering friends. We went to church on Wednesdays, attended inspiring Christian rock concerts, and sang songs of praise to God as we traveled back and forth to the performances. I was deeply grateful not to be alone all the time. When I would fall away for a short time, I would hear a tap on my door late at night, and that same small group would come plead with me to start anew. We'd sit outside under the stars and share dreams of who we hoped to become. Then we would pray, asking God for strength so I could place my life firmly in His hands.

I moved into a safe, loving house with a friend in recovery, determined to live abundantly in God's grace, and become the woman He created me to be.

Along the way, I landed a job at Houston's, one of the nicer restaurants in the area.

My first day on the job changed my life forever – January 6th. I remember being very nervous as my trainer, Rachel, hovered over my shoulder.

I welcomed a table of ten men and asked for their drink order. The guys began teasing their friend Chris, who was sitting in the corner wearing a white T-shirt emblazoned with a fishing symbol. He seemed shy, and I thought he was kind of cute.

His friends urged him to flirt with my trainer, Rachel. "Forget Rachel, who's the blonde?" he replied.

I blushed and walked away.

Chris came in on a regular basis from then on, and he saw to it I was always his server. We engaged in sparkling conversation. He definitely bought more $35 steaks than (I later learned) his budget allowed. Although the flirtation was enjoyable, I tried to make it clear to him I had recently broken up with someone. The reality was I secretly felt that if he knew the truth about me, he would lose interest. But Chris was persistent and kept coming back.

We spoke a few times on the phone before he finally asked me out for the first time, a breakfast date. I assumed that he had lots of money, since he seemed to have no problem eating at Houston's so often. I previously had such nice cars that I didn't want him to see the simple little Toyota I now drove; it embarrassed me.

I also didn't want him seeing where I lived, since I was rooming with people in recovery. He didn't know my secret yet. The embarrassment over my car and living conditions left me behaving rather elusively, so I arranged to meet him at the restaurant.

Finally, when Chris asked me out on our first real evening date, I had to come clean and tell him where I lived. He didn't flinch; he just came and picked me up. I wasn't sure I wanted to date him because we seemed so different on the outside. He drove a truck and enjoyed hunting, loved country music, always wore cowboy boots, was a construction superintendent, and was proud to describe himself as an "outdoorsman." I had never met or dated anyone with those interests. I saw myself dating a man who drove a BMW, worked in corporate America, loved social events, and dreamed of traveling to exotic places.

However, Chris slowly melted my resistance. When I mentioned my favorite musician was Natalie Merchant, that sweet man went to the trouble of calling a radio station and asking, "Who is Natalie Merchant and where do I get her CDs?" That night, he brought me a CD along with a beautiful white rose from his garden.

He was a very charming, laid-back guy – a true gentleman. We went on six dates before he tried to kiss me goodnight. It had been a long time since I had dated someone as genuinely nice and kind as Chris. My fear of rejection and my hidden drug problem, however, kept me from fully embracing the connection we had. I promised myself to never give my heart away to another man. Chris was a little standoffish, too, probably because he had been burned by a marriage that ended badly.

I didn't mind his caution, because it meant I didn't have to be fully emotionally involved with him. He never quite knew where I was or what I was doing. I always had an "out." When making plans with him, I would say, "Okay, let's spend time together until two. But at three o'clock, I have this thing I have to do."

I kept him at arm's length until the day I realized my feelings had changed. After bike riding, we stopped at the health food store and suddenly it hit me -- I didn't want to leave. I didn't need an "out" anymore. I realized I liked Chris so much that my fear was disappearing.

We were driving in his truck one Saturday afternoon when I found myself saying, "I don't really want this date to end." He responded, "Why don't I drop you off, you can get ready, and I can take you to dinner?" Then he smiled.

For the next four months, the feelings intensified. We rode bikes, went to the movies, ate at nice restaurants, and took long walks along Delray Beach's Atlantic Avenue, where we shared ice cream and coffee. We laughed a lot, and shared thoughts and ideals and dreams that mattered to us. We traveled to the Florida Keys and went bike riding along sandy shores. We took his boat out and spent hours wading in the blue waters off Singer Island. We were the picture of romance. We began to open up about our desires and fears. And in the process, we became best friends.

Chris began to know me for who I was -- and loved me anyway. He saw the best in me. The first truly romantic thing Chris said to me was, "I am not sure whose prayers were answered when we met... mine or yours." I asked myself if this could be real love. I moved again, into an apartment in a beautiful complex with a female roommate, which was another sign of my growth and well-being. When my parents offered me a job with their real estate company, I jumped at the chance to use my marketing skills again, and moved up to Orlando.

Chris and I continued to see each other. We didn't want 150 miles' distance between the two cities to stop us, so every weekend I drove down and spent it with him, or he rode up to be with me.

Eventually, it was time to meet Chris's daughter Olivia, a tiny brunette with tons of hair and big brown eyes. I really wanted her to love me because I was really digging her dad. I called my best friend, Alex, and said, "I don't know what to say to this little girl."

"Things will be fine," she reassured. "She's going to show you her boo-boos, and tell you about school, and say all the things little kids say. Talk to Olivia like you talk to my kids."

Chris and I set up a situation, pretending to accidentally meet while he was spending time with Olivia on Singer Island – the accidental/on purpose run-in. It worked like a charm and Olivia, who just turned seven, asked me to join them for dinner. Olivia and I sat alongside the ocean seawall, pointing out fish and giggling as the sun set in front of us.

Later, while waiting for the valet to bring around his truck, Chris asked Olivia, "Hey, do you mind if Mary Jane rides home with us?"

I nervously stood there while Olivia didn't answer her dad. The valet pulled up in the truck. Chris looked at me, shrugging, unsure of what to do. But just before Olivia climbed in, she tapped me on the arm and said, "Come on. The truck's here. We gotta go!"

I was so relieved she liked me. My heart melted when she invited me to come along. We had a good time on the ride home and that led to a series of meet-ups – going to the movies, nights at the pizza place – things we could enjoy together. Olivia got to know me and I really enjoyed her company. Her sweet nature was another gift God gave me. Without children of my own, I had never really received this kind of love from a child. A child's love is different from the love of an adult, friend, or a parent. Olivia's kindness gave me hope that I could accept love again and trust that I was worthy of good things. Olivia taught me to have confidence in intimate, loving relationships. Because she lived with Chris, I learned how to care for a child, which included making huge sacrifices. My feelings for Olivia gave me a chance to practice giving without expecting anything in return. I was unaware how selfish I had become. As the only daughter in my family, treated like a child with a handicap for so long, *I* was the one who received the care. Rarely in my life did I have the opportunity to give instead of receive.

As I played the role of a mother, the desire to give her a wonderful life began to resonate in my heart. It slowly transformed me.

Though Olivia and Chris became a ray of sunshine in my new life, I couldn't shake the darkness of my old life. I continued to use drugs sporadically and secretively, fearing Chris or Olivia might catch on. Chris suspected, but never really put all of the pieces together. My behavior was odd at times. Sometimes I came down for the weekend and chose to stay at a hotel instead of his house.

"Why is your schedule so ambiguous?" he asked. "I called you three days ago and you haven't returned my message."

Chris, the sweet trusting man that he was, just didn't get it. However, my mom, deceived by me many times before, could see right through my secretive behavior. She adds:

I had to fire Mary Jane a couple of times because she lied to us. I thought she was doing drugs because she wouldn't pick up the phone when I called her, and she would miss work. Firing my own daughter was incredibly awkward but usually she managed to talk her way back into a job. She was an incredible negotiator and being her mom, I was her safety net.

The amazing thing was that everybody thought Mary Jane was absolutely the best person for the job. She was in charge of public relations and she did some phenomenal things working for us. She would create successful radio and media campaigns that would generate new business and drive traffic into our office. She and her dad started a charity for children whose parents were in the service defending our country overseas. Mary Jane raised thousands of dollars while she got the local media to adopt the charity. Thousands of toys were donated to support military families. The National Guard gave her a medal of honor.

But one time I was out of town with our partners and I called the office, but Mary Jane wasn't there. I just knew she was using again. It was a couple days before I could track her down.

With my parents catching on to my drug use, it was only a matter of time before they fired me permanently and sent me to rehab again. I decided a move back to West Palm Beach would be the healthiest choice for me; then Chris invited me to move in with him and his daughter. We wanted to take our relationship to next level and were tired of the long-distance commute. For Olivia's sake, I moved into the guest bedroom. I didn't want to confuse her by staying in Chris's room. We told her it was just temporary. I looked for apartments but couldn't find an affordable one.

We fought about our living situation. I didn't want to live with Chris without being engaged or, better yet, married. I knew God wanted more for Chris and me. I was so convinced marriage was the Divine plan, I decided to attend Chris's non-denominational church. I was shocked. Unlike the reserved Catholic masses I was used to, this was a charismatic fellowship. Catholics never raised their hands or expressed faith in such a magnetic, external way. On my first visit, people spoke in tongues during the service. I sat in the pew, thinking, *What is that? Are people speaking in their native languages?* I just thought it was really odd.

I had never heard music like the stuff they were singing that morning. At my church in Orlando, I learned a lot of praise and worship songs but this was lively gospel music. People waved their hands in the air. A woman next to Chris and me clapped her hands and said "Hallelujah, amen!"

I kept waiting for someone to tell her to be quiet because she was interrupting the service. It was really strange for me, but I eventually became used to it. This church later became my saving grace, and the path which led me to a greater relationship with the Holy Spirit.

CHAPTER EIGHTEEN

Even though Chris and I were happy in our relationship, the sharp teeth of addiction continued to gnaw at my soul. Months of wonderful sobriety, during which I built strong work and family relationships, came crashing down when I succumbed to the drug demon once more. I was careful to never bring drugs around Olivia -- at least I knew enough not to inflict my problems on an innocent child.

When Chris went away on hunting trips, Olivia stayed at her mother's house. Chris usually left on a Friday afternoon. I didn't enjoy staying home alone in such a big house, so I told him I would spend the weekend at Kerrie's place. In reality, I began checking myself into hotels like the Hampton Inn Suites or the Ritz Carlton.

I looked like any other professional businesswoman dressed in a blazer and skirt, rolling my luggage bag into the lobby of a beautifully decorated hotel. But unlike others, inside my suitcase would be a stash of cocaine, crack, downers, and beer. These were the tools I felt I needed to hibernate for the weekend.

After smoking crack all night in my hotel room, my head was clear enough in the morning to write down my thoughts, even do a little poetry writing.

The birds chirping outside the window were a bittersweet sound: It brought the assurance I made it through another long night, but also a sledgehammer of regret that I had wasted another precious day of life. I tried to make up for it by jotting down my thoughts. I figured that if I wrote a book that helped other people, my life wouldn't have been completely pointless. The fact that I was writing a book about addiction *while still doing drugs* was a distinction lost on me at that time.

One morning, I wrote:

My mind travels beyond places that are routine or common. I find myself thinking about traveling spiritually. I am a bit frightened because I have almost accepted the possibility that I may be one of God's creations meant to serve as a (cautionary???) lesson to others. I am no longer sure if I was meant to be the one out of thirty-six who will survive addiction.

I am tired of my drug habit and the life I live. My life is a series of "new beginnings" (jobs, homes, rules) and quite frankly, I would rather be with Christ. It is almost as if part of the "spirit of crack" has made a home in my flesh. The first time my lips wrapped around the glass pipe, and the smoke bled from my lungs and moved through my veins, the destructive force began its mission to possess me in my thoughts, body, and mind. Since that night I was introduced to crack, I began to lose any sense of my feelings. Most of the time I am neutral, experiencing no intense emotions – not much anger, nothing explosive in my relationships with men and my friendships with girlfriends, no real joy or exuberance either. I've become a walking shell.

My mind knows spiritual truths beyond the five senses. I've seen the demonic faces that travel in the darkness, looking for someone to attach themselves to. I see their faces amongst the trees and I have gone from fear of them to noting them as they appear. I know I am protected from harm because of Christ.

When I look in the mirror I see an attractive woman who is a slave. I've allowed my temple to deteriorate. My hands and feet have become gray and old-looking and my eyes have lost the purity of the little girl who wants out! Where I was once an endless source of adrenaline, enthusiasm, and focused goals, I am now a fearful liar. I no longer have the same inner worthiness I once had.

I believe crack was intentionally created, by those who have no God, to seek and destroy as many as possible – not just the suffering addict, but the lives of parents who must watch their child suffer, lose everything over and over again, struggle to rebuild their lives, and then start another cycle of active addiction. It's a domino effect that knocks out one child at a time. It also takes down one family at a time as they, too, lose hope.

I am writing this book to educate you on addiction -- living an intentionally sinful life apart from God, and walking a superficially spiritual existence -- to warn you about what you may have to deal with. But mostly, I write this to satisfy one of the reasons I was created.

I need to warn all those with a curious nature: Ask God to spare you from this life of highs and lows, of too many losses of friends, career choices, lovers, and dreams. It's not called the "slave drug" for nothing. When the energy of crack unfolds within your soul, a clash of forces takes place. You will begin to behave in a way you know is wrong. Once the energy dies and you come in touch with your soul again, the guilt will overwhelm you. This is the clashing.

I got tired of journaling my thoughts in that form, so I switched to writing a poem on the back of the hotel stationary.

Tick tock...Tick tock
The clock above me whispers
"Time to go home"
Say the hands upon the wall
My addiction tells me "Never"

The voice of crack
Shouts to me
"Mary Jane, please don't go"

One day, two days, three days, a week
When will this cycle stop?

Guilt, Shame and Fear
Cloud my perceptions
Now, addiction roars
"Come to me, my child, and fear no more"

I run full speed
Never looking back
To see the destruction
To feel what I have lost

Then, a light
Dim at first
Catches my attention ... I watch

"Trust in me"
Said God above
"For you are my child, I will protect and love"

Then angels He sent
From heaven above
And the Holy Spirit fills me with love

He then took my hand
And together we walk towards
The Promised Land

I stumble behind
He patiently waits
For He knows in my heart
I seek what is right.

I rested quietly, almost peacefully, in my bed for a little while. Hotels are busy places early in the morning, buzzing with all the activity of a new day. Businessmen and women check out, kids run down the hallway, and I realized I was no longer the only one up.

So much fear ran through my veins. My chest tightened up and I feared the worst. "Am I going to die from a heart attack?" I asked myself.

I called Chris to report my condition. He was heading to work but agreed to turn his truck around and come get me. I hung up the phone and realized how far away he was. There was no way he would rescue me in time.

I was sure I would be dead by the time he arrived, so I opened the door. Still in pajamas, I made my way to the elevator. Once the door opened in the lobby I faced a group of clean, well-groomed guests. They smiled politely and I attempted to make small talk.

Making my way to the couch near the door, I asked a stranger to hold my hand. My chest still pounded irregularly and I felt tightness in my breathing.

"Where is your family?" the elderly man inquired.

"Please call 9-1-1," I muttered. "I may be having a heart attack." An onlooker called emergency services and another called Chris again on my cell.

The paramedics arrived within a short time and jumped into action, asking me questions about my health. I lied to them. "It's nothing," I said. "I was fighting with my boyfriend. I'm probably just stressed." They said my blood pressure was running a bit high but that was all they could detect.

"Probably just anxiety," one medical worker surmised. I tried to dismiss them as quickly as possible, worried about whether or not the police get called in this kind of emergency.

Fortunately, the police were not summoned. The paramedics released me and I hustled back through the lobby to the elevator doors. I was utterly embarrassed, but managed to call Chris again. When he picked up the phone, I tried to weasel out of it but he insisted I come home. He wanted a promise, a guarantee; I would never use drugs again. Naturally I said, "Never again. This is the last time." At that moment, I meant it – I always meant it. I made Chris dozens of promises over the three years we dated. In heated conversations, I would promise to try harder to be a woman he could be proud to date. However, because I had untreated addiction, I would randomly disappear for hours or days at a time. Upon my return, he was incredibly disappointed in my behavior. We would argue, make up, and I would swear that I would change. The drama of the morning caused my high to wear off, so I told Chris I would just drive myself home and meet him at the house. He agreed. I ran back up to the room and threw my belongings in my suitcase, then rushed to the parking lot. I wanted to beat him home so I could have some time to hop in the shower and clean up a bit. Maybe if I looked beautiful when he arrived home, it would ease the tension. Perhaps making love would show Chris that I truly loved him, despite my actions. Maybe he would see me as a victim of this terrible addiction, and not a worthless woman without hope.

CHAPTER NINETEEN

Spiritually, I knew I shouldn't be living with a man who wasn't my husband. It was killing me and I felt the Holy Spirit's conviction that we were committing the sin of living together outside of marriage. Chris promised he would propose by Christmas, even claiming he had the ring.

We spent the holidays with my parents and I really thought it was going to happen then. Mom and Dad wanted to renew their vows. My dad re-proposed to my mom. They were crying; we were crying. It seemed like the perfect opportunity for Chris to ask me for my hand in marriage. It was Christmas and I thought, *now it's my turn.* But the proposal didn't come.

Though it was a joyous occasion for my family, I was an emotional wreck. Trying to keep it together, I walked to the back of my parent's house for some privacy. My dad entered the room and shut the door. "Look, I know why you're upset," he said, "Chris has asked for your hand in marriage and I've given him permission. It's going to be soon. Just hold on."

For two hours I cried silently as Chris and I drove back to West Palm Beach. Once we arrived home, I was finally ready to speak. "You promised! How could you do this?" I cried. "I would have moved out six or eight months ago so you could have your space. I just can't live like this anymore."

"It's not your fault, it's my fault. I'm a procrastinator," he said; I didn't know whether to be relieved or infuriated that he didn't have a better reason. He promised he would make it up to me.

A month later Chris finally kept his promise, and against my sponsor's advice, I said, "yes."

The year of our engagement was challenging. I relapsed once, but Chris stuck with me. I wasn't sure why. He just said he saw the best in me.

I really tried to be super step-mom and super wife-to-be. I overproduced at work and brought home money to help pay the bills. I went to recovery meetings and did my step work faithfully. I felt invincible. But, at that time, six months seemed to be my record for sobriety.

CHAPTER TWENTY

While it still felt like the relationship with my mom was irreparable, I certainly wanted to try improving things with my dad. After years of putting him through the hell of my addiction, I knew I needed to make amends. A.A.'s Ninth Step is, "Make direct amends to such people wherever possible, except when to do so would injure them or others."

Following that suggestion, I sat down and penned this letter to my father.

∿

Dear Dad,

This letter comes to you from the heart, and with the invitation that Christ would be among you and I as we sit down to talk. This is a sacramental letter, when you consider that my hope is to become closer to you by knocking down all the doubt and distrust that may be blocking us from a mature relationship and, of course, a right relation to God.

I can't tell you the hundreds of times I have wanted to tell you how sorry I have been for my actions during my active addiction. Yet, this step I am attempting to take with you goes far beyond the words, "I am sorry." To "amend" means to "make right" or to "add to." And until I seriously worked the first eight steps, I would not be able to honestly and clearly see my part. I also did not have the courage to tell you what I have done, out of fear of losing you. The shame was too great for me to admit until now.

I am sure most of what I am about to confess, you already know in your heart. Yet my desire is to start fresh with you. My goal is to, one day at a time, earn your trust in my life and in my words. I am willing to take the chance right now, in order that you and I have nothing standing between us to prevent our growing as father and daughter.

While I was high on crack, I took things out of the garage that did not belong to me. At that moment, I was a total slave to crack cocaine. It was deceitful and wrong. I handled the situation to meet only my addictive needs.

When you trusted me in your home, I used drugs in my room. That was self-seeking and inconsiderate. Even though you weren't there, it endangered your peaceful home life. I know now the full extent of that effect. I created a wedge between you and I on a spiritual level.

There were times I lied to protect you from my terrifying truth. Yet there were other times when I lied intentionally, so you would meet me and help me buy food so I could eat that day.

I take full responsibility for all the chaos I have caused in your heart, and all of the torment in your soul. I hope you can, and will, forgive me for all the nights you did not sleep for fear of finding me dead. I want you to know that the young child within me wanted to be close to you always, Papa. Yet I was so entrenched in my disease, I was unable to make any other choice at that time. I know today how difficult it must have been to see me so thin and so scared.

Even now as I write this I cry, because I can see what my addiction has done. Visiting your sick and dying daughter in treatment must have made you question your faith in Christ and again, I hope you can forgive me for causing you even a moment of doubt in our God. I am so sorry you had to come and look for me in crack town late in the evenings. I am sure that I have also made your relationship with Mom even more challenging at times. In looking back, I see all the destruction my addiction and my disease caused you over the last few years.

Can you give me another sober chance to earn your respect?

I am committed to living right. I am dedicated to change. I am never going to give up on myself, and I will not allow crack to destroy me spiritually and physically. My hope in writing this letter is to show you that I, too, know and feel the sting of my choices. I take full responsibility for hurting you. I am aware of what I have done, and what I have failed to do.

I will never forget the afternoon we sat in the living room, and I told you how lost I was. I begged you to never let go of me, and you never have. I know I am alive and well because you never quit praying for me. Your love and grace give me the freedom to continue to try and recover completely. I am practicing the surrender process every day.

And one more thing, Dad. I am willing to answer any questions you may have, and take this new journey at a pace you are okay with. Thank you for being my father, and the other half of my two best friends.

Mary Jane

～

My dad shares his feelings about that time:

Leigh was always a bigger influence in Mary Jane's life than I was. I was a student and worked full-time when Mary Jane was born up until she was three-and-a-half years old.

Once I was gone to a training class in Atlanta for three weeks and the day before I was scheduled to come back home Mary Jane finally asked Leigh, 'Where's Daddy?'

My early memory of fatherhood was that of Mary Jane sitting on my lap as I was studying. She had an inquisitive nature and liked to push us – well, Leigh, especially – to the edge. That was just her personality. As my first child, I didn't really know if every kid was like that or just Mary Jane.

But Chad came along and he was completely the opposite – one hundred and eighty degrees. Even in grade school, she pushed to go beyond where we wanted her to go. She thought she was ready for everything in life and she wasn't.

I was way too passive in addressing my daughter's addiction issues. I put my head in the sand and hoped it would go away, but of course, that's not the way it works. When Chad would tell us he had troubles of any kind, I took it more seriously. Why I took that response to him and not with Mary Jane, I don't know... Maybe I couldn't believe Mary Jane's drugs in and of themselves weren't as big of a deal to me.

I grew up in the bar my Dad owned. My whole life I saw alcoholics around me and maybe I became desensitized to it. Those people came in and got so drunk they couldn't make it home. But then the next day, sure enough, they came back to the bar as if nothing bad had happened. It didn't seem to have an impact on them so maybe that's why I had a more laid-back attitude toward substance addiction.

The moment I finally knew I needed to address Mary Jane's issues was in church. She was sitting next to me, strung out, and I began to experience a strange feeling all over my body. I began praying hard and it was clear God was talking to me.

"What am I going to do?" I began asking. "This isn't good. What's going to happen to my daughter? What's next?" I knew at that point it was going to be a long journey.

Leigh had her friend Marti to talk to and she spent every weekend with her. She would be gone for two or three days. I think maybe that was her relief valve. But I had nobody outside of Leigh. I didn't want to tell family members. I didn't want anybody to think poorly of Mary Jane even though, in hindsight, they probably already knew.

Eventually, I found out someone I was close to had similar issues with his son. He was hiding the same internal things I was fighting and we didn't know it. I finally learned of it when he happened to be at our house and got a call about his son.

When we discovered we were facing the same issues as parents of addicts we were able to sit for hours and talk about all of the turmoil, headaches, and heartaches. I felt relieved to know there was somebody else facing the same issues. There was somebody I could call when I needed to talk.

CHAPTER TWENTY-ONE

My mom weighs in with her thoughts on what it was like to be my mother during the chaos of my lost years.

From day one Mary Jane never heard the word "no." Everything was always a negotiation with her. Joe would come home from work and she would be crying in one chair; I was crying in another chair because we butted heads all day. Mary Jane wanted to see the world from a young age, and be out with friends all the time; I wanted her to slow down. She just always brought out the worst in me by wanting to participate in activities that I wasn't sure she was old enough to do.

She also brought out the best in me, too. She and I have had so many wonderful memories together. She would ask Dad and me to attend all her cheerleading events and social events. She loved having Joe and I around. As she went off to college, she invited us to come to all her UCF games, all her sorority parent-student weekends, along with the UCF alumni activities so we could meet her friends. After college, as Mary Jane became a successful marketing representative, she made sure we had VIP tickets to jazz concerts, dinner shows, and community events. We have spent hundreds of hours arm in arm on the shores of beautiful beaches and walking along sidewalks during holidays, looking inside store windows. She and I have an incredible bond. There have been more fun days than sad days, for sure. Mary Jane was never smart around me. She never cursed at me, or used foul language, she was just born with an ambition to be on the go all the time. It wasn't bad behavior externally, it was just inward. From the minute she arrived [in this world] her head turned up and down and right and left. There was activity from that moment on. She was always afraid she was going to miss something. I heard that the firstborn would sleep all the time and Mary Jane didn't get that message -- she didn't read that book.

Early in middle school, she left her bike in our neighbor's driveway and they accidentally backed over it. Naturally, I was upset and grounded her to her room. I don't remember how long she was up there when I heard screaming and shouting – apparently from outside our house. I ran out the front door to find Mary Jane leaning out the window of her bedroom. She had removed the screen and was hollering to anyone who would listen, "My mom doesn't love me! Somebody help me! I need to be rescued!" Listening to her that day made me chuckle. She was always so dramatic.

When she was a junior in high school and we were having one of our heated discussions, I dropped to my knees and began looking under the sofa. She asked what I was doing and I told her I was looking for the instructions. "I know God would not send you to me without the instructions" I shouted. Then we stopped arguing and both cried and had a good belly laugh. We were two strong-willed women who knew how to push each other's buttons.

Drugs eventually took everything from her. Our lives were shattered by it. I devoted every bit of energy to "fixing" her addiction, but I also had my own life to keep in order. We had a real estate business and people depended on us. We had obligations to them as well. I couldn't just quit my job and tend to every need of my adult children.

When Joe and I started that business, we decided that it would be God-centered. In real estate, that's odd, but we wanted to run a loving, caring organization. Joe and I worked hard on it every single day. It was our rock.

When Mary Jane called at three in the morning, it was for help. God must have it set up that as a parent you never run out of unconditional love – because she really pushed us to the limit.

I started attending therapy for families of drug abusers. Joe couldn't go as much because the stories that other parents and loved ones shared were so sad it would take your breath away, but I went to the meetings because I thought I could help Mary Jane. I'm her mom and I felt I should be able to put a stop to this! But I learned I couldn't stop the train. It goes at such a speed toward that wall you just can't prevent the crash.

The people at the meetings tried to teach me how to let go, though I never did that completely. At one point around this time, I wrote a little note to my daughter:

∽

"Dear Mary Jane,

I will practice letting go. I will work to understand that your actions don't control me and that I cannot control your actions. I will work on more love, less fear. I will say a prayer for both of us every day that we will have the courage to change the things we can.

I love you, Mom"

∽

Joe and I felt alone, as if there was no one we could speak to other than each other. We had been lying to our friends and covering up for our child. We wanted to protect our kids and keep them from being judged and it felt like our friends would never have understood the situation.

I did have one friend, Marti, to whom I opened up. She was dying of cancer, the disease she had battled for eight years. I regularly visited her bedside in Saint Pete and eventually told her what I was going through with my daughter. Two weeks before she passed on, Marti grabbed my hand and said, "As bad as it is for me, I wouldn't trade places with you, honey."

Marti and Mary Jane were very connected and very close to one another. Marti knew Mary Jane was literally fighting for her life. They would spend hours on the phone together sharing their battles with two very different diseases; however, they knew that prayer and petition would bring some peace. They would laugh about funny things they did together when Mary Jane was growing up. Before Marti died, she called Mary Jane one last time to share her respect for Mary Jane's diligence to keep fighting. Mary Jane told me they cried as Marti told her how she knew that addiction was far worse than cancer because of the perception of being an addict. She begged Mary Jane to keep trying and one day, she too would have peace. They never spoke again.

When Marti died, Mary Jane was strung-out and missed the funeral. Things like that made me angry but I always blamed Satan. No one else could have that kind of control over my strong-willed daughter. More times than I can recall, I prayed out loud in my car or home. I screamed out to the Devil – in the name of Jesus Christ – to let her go.

Joe's biggest fear was that Mary Jane would die and he would lose me. He felt that I might also die, just from the pain of losing my child.

The only thing that kept us together was our belief in God.

Both my mother and I were blessed with Marti's presence in our lives. To this day, I still remember Marti and my last conversation before she died. I was sitting on a couch watching television in a well-groomed women's halfway house on a Friday night when the phone rang. On the other end, Marti's lively voice asked, "Whatcha doing, babe?" We talked for an hour about our spiritual journeys. Marti's journey included chemo treatments, bouts of throwing up for days at a time, a lack of appetite, and anger about her looming death. Yet she still continued to fight the bone cancer growing rampant through her body. She was pissed knowing there wasn't a damn thing she could do about it. Through this anger, she still found the patience to counsel me through sharing the Bible readings she was studying, and how she was finding the courage to say goodbye to her two daughters, Stacey and Deanna. She shared how she came to peace with death itself; however, the source of her anger was missing watching her two lovely daughters growing up.

Even on her deathbed, Marti reminded me I still had a fighting chance against my disease. She gently pleaded with me to never, ever give up. She reminded me how much she loved me and how proud she was to have known me. She whispered that I was the only person in her world who knew what it was like to fight to stay alive because both of us had stared the Angel of Death squarely in the face several times. We both stood at the crossroads asking ourselves, "Do I fight or do I give in?"

Marti and I shared one other common trait: the unwavering love for our families because, some days, that love was the only thing motivating us to keep fighting like hell so we could spend one more precious day with them.

I didn't know that evening was the last time I would hear Marti's familiar voice; otherwise, I would have kept her on the phone longer, asking her to share her secrets on living with abundance, grace, and courage.

What I did learn, from watching Marti walk through her challenges, was how to be a woman of God and hold His hand no matter where He led her.

CHAPTER TWENTY-TWO

Four years after Marti passed away, I said, "I do" and walked down the aisle. Something I rarely watch is the video of my wedding to Chris. It's still a very painful memory and is difficult to write about it in this book, even today. However, in the spirit of full disclosure, I knew God's unconditional love and faithfulness would be revealed if I allowed you to see *inside* my most painful memory. This sorrow is far beyond being deaf as a little girl and the ridicule I endured. It is more painful than the kidnapping and the gunshot wound, or the ten years of intermittent addiction. I prayed for courage to share this story so that you would see that God does heal even the deepest wounds and regrets. I never spoke about it to anyone; it's still too raw at this point in my life. Until now.

Unlike my ragtag first wedding, where I showed up in a tank top and Capri pants, I was determined this second wedding was going to be the ceremony I dreamed of as a little girl. Even though I met Chris at a steakhouse instead of a royal ball, I knew I had found my Prince Charming. Living a sober life was shaping up to be pretty perfect. Looking back, I realize my fatal flaw was not that I didn't invite God into my life, but that I still instructed Him about where and when he could be present. As those of us in recovery say, I was the epitome of "self-will run riot." I appeared to bending to God's will, yet internally I was barking orders as to how I wanted my life to be orchestrated.

We had every detail perfectly planned. It was important to us that close family and friends played an integral role. The flower arrangements were handmade by special friends; the tender wedding scriptures from the book of Corinthians and Psalms were especially selected to include God's promises for marriage, and were read by my godmother and best companions. The reception included family favorite polka songs. The church was beautifully decorated with fresh flowers, candelabras, and dim lighting.

The ambiance inside the hotel ballroom was exquisite with gold tapered candles, fine linen tablecloths, and tailored chair covers. Instead of table numbers, we labeled each with attributes of a successful marriage: ambition, passion, commitment, and love. I wanted every guest to feel as though they were the bride and groom. The church service was in dim lighting, and I deliberately chose a small cathedral so each guest could hear the exchange of our vows.

As the guests inside awaited the service, the bridal party was lined up, two by two, waiting for the music to begin. I was in the back of the church, anxiously poised to walk up the aisle when I heard the wedding song play. As I stepped out of the bridal room and turned the corner, our eyes met: my father's and mine. His face flushed with surprise at the beauty of his little girl, all grown up and dressed in white lace and shimmering crystal beadwork. Tears welled up in his eyes, and his chest expanded, as though to catch his breath. I gracefully walked towards him, smiling with excitement and pure joy. I tenderly reached out to him with gratitude, and felt overwhelmed with adoration for the man who stood by my side. My dad was an integral part of my life in each victory and was a strong spiritual warrior in moments of distress. From this day forward, he would no longer be the sole man in my life. He would hand me over to another whom I would love deeply. He, too, was overcome with emotion. We both gained our composure and walked down the aisle, elated this day had finally come.

The service was everything Chris and I planned. The church procession went exactly as hoped. I felt like God was asked to bless our marriage. Olivia, Chris, and I took our vows as a family. The wedding reception was high energy and love-filled. We were introduced to our guests as husband and wife, and I was happier than I had ever been. We danced our first song to Marc Cohn's *True Companion* and I knew I was safe in Chris's arms. The traditional wedding toasts were sincere. To have so many there in honor of our relationship was sacred.

Chris and I made rounds to the tables and welcomed every guest. I spent most of the night with family, dancing to our favorite tunes.

In a naive act of goodwill, I made the mistake of inviting some of the people from my past to our wedding. There were four people I never should have considered extending an invitation. I fooled myself into thinking they were friends who deserved to witness my special day, because once I decided to get sober they supported my decision. There they were, smiling and cheering as I danced around in my white gown. But what happened next reawakened the demon of addiction within.

After dancing with my husband, I sipped on my ginger ale.Chris and I took a seat in front of the room, along with the bridal party. My father got up to toast us, told funny stories from my childhood, and shared his quirky jokes about what it takes to have a successful marriage. His attention turned to Chris. "As my new so- in-law, you should know the two words that have saved my marriage — and created harmony between Leigh and I for more than thirty years — will also save you from having disputes with Mary Jane. When it doubt Chris, simply look at Mary Jane and say 'Yes, dear' and quickly walk away." The 250 guests cheered and laughed aloud.

Suddenly, my attention was pulled from my dad's speech when a waiter set two flutes of in front of us. The waiter discreetly pointed out that one glass was ginger ale and the other was champagne. My father continued to tell a quirky story about me as a child, but I could not laugh along with the guests. My attention was no longer on my new husband or my dear father, but on the two identical glasses in front of me. The only way I can describe it is the room faded away, and those glasses came into sharp focus. Like Alice in *Through the Looking-Glass*, sipping from one would keep me there, sober and jovial, the perfect bride with my perfect husband; the other foretold broken promises and shattered dreams. With six months of sobriety behind me, I justified the drink by telling myself it was <u>my</u> wedding and I deserved it for all my hard work.

Most of the night was picture-perfect, and I managed to limit myself to, only a few drinks. However, my memory gets blurry later in the evening. For that reason, I'll let my friends and family members share their recollections of my wedding.

Kerrie says:

The party was going fine. It wasn't until the end of the reception when Mary Jane came into the reception hall and said something bizarre to the girl sitting next to me, something like "I've got toilet paper stuck to my dress." I looked at the girl and shrugged.

[I then realized] Mary Jane was high. It was so obvious. She was very uninhibited. What started with a very beautiful woman dressed in wedding gown turned into a night of make-up running down a bride's face as she slurred her words. The beautiful woman had disappeared and the disease was what we saw.

When I saw Mary Jane like that, I felt like she would never make it out of addiction alive. If you can't make it through your own wedding reception, I thought...

Chris weighs in what he saw:

At the reception, she and I went around to everybody's tables laughing, celebrating and having a wonderful time as husband and wife. Then, towards the end of the evening as guests were leaving, I just noticed she went from good to bad, and downhill fast. I asked her, "Who gave you something? Did you take drugs?" There were a handful of strange people from her past that I didn't know and I started to suspect one of them had put something in her drink. I sure hoped it was somebody else and not Mary Jane's choice.

My friend Kerrie adds:

Chris had to help Mary Jane up to their room. Minutes later, he called Alex, the girl I was sitting with, and asked for help. Mary Jane was having some kind of attack and he was terrified. I guess he thought it was a panic attack. Poor guy.

Alex ran up to their room and I followed her. When I got to the room, I could just see the sickness in her. Mary Jane was lying on the bed.

There was a weird aura in the room but I focused on keeping her conscious. It was a very sad ending to a very beautiful day.

I remember being inside the honeymoon suite crying because I couldn't figure out what went wrong. I had only had one glass of champagne. I went into the bathroom and found my dress in a wrinkled heap on the floor. *How can this be happening to me?* I asked myself. No matter how much I tried to snap out of it and regain my composure, the "mind rush" would not stop and the room spun out of control. If I lay very still, I could remain calm. I remember Kerrie, Alex, and Chris asking me questions about how this happened. I honestly did not know. It was another moment in which I wished I was dead. A drink or two did not create that kind of high; the feeling was overwhelming and terrifying. I couldn't regain concentration; my eyesight was blurry and out-of-focus. I was lying on my back and I can remember seeing distorted faces leaning over me, trying to keep me conscious by asking me questions. "What is your name? Do you know where you are? Who gave you something?" I did not know the answer to the last question. The four so-called supporters from my past may not have been so supportive after all. It appeared all my hard work towards recovery and a new life was ending badly. By taking that first glass of champagne, had I set this nightmare in motion? Was this my punishment for choosing drink over sobriety?

My mom backtracks to the last time she saw me that night:

Towards the end of the reception, she left. She didn't say goodbye and you could tell she was out of it. Chris took her out of the room. I don't think she could stand up at that point and that's when I knew something had happened.

The wedding cost around twenty-five thousand dollars. We had twenty-seven rooms at the beautiful Embassy Suites for our family who had flown in from all over the country. At first, people assumed the bride had gone upstairs to change her clothes, but the next morning, she didn't show up for the breakfast reception. "Where's Mary Jane?" people kept asking.

I would not lie for her. I just shrugged and said, "Who knows, I haven't seen her yet. Maybe she's sleeping it off."

Eventually Chris came downstairs and said Mary Jane would not be joining us.

Kerrie again:

Chris just said, "She's tired." He was carrying the weight of the world on his shoulders. I felt so bad for him. I know what I felt like as her friend, and couldn't imagine what he felt like as a new groom. This was how the marriage was starting off?

I never did see her that morning; I knew she wouldn't want to. I had breakfast alone and couldn't wait to get out of there. Ready to bolt, I said my goodbyes to the people I knew and headed to the car.

The first thing I did on my way out of Orlando was to put on some Christian music. I thought it would take me out of this suffocating hold I felt. But even worship music didn't work. It wasn't until a day and a half later that it finally lifted. That was the last time I've ever felt like that. I know that it was demons. If you could picture the vortex of a tornado and how it spins around, picture in that vortex demons flying at a high speed and that's what it felt like. I prayed over Mary Jane and Chris because I knew this was bigger than I imagined and they couldn't handle it without God. Once again, Mary Jane was fighting for her spiritual and physical life. This setback was more spiritual than physical. There was a dark, evil curse following her.

My mom spoke to Chris after the humiliating events of our wedding. She explains:

Chris called us two weeks after the wedding ceremony. We wanted to protect him and his daughter. Mary Jane had the keys to his home, his checkbook -- all the things she needed to turn his life upside down. I wouldn't wish that on anybody. We told him whatever he needed to do, we were with him. Chris knew he had our support in helping him any way we could. We suggested he change the locks and do all the things we had to do over the years.

There's a wedding photo in her guest room to this day, and I usually turn it over because I can't bear to look at it. My sweet daughter, so drugged and out of it on her wedding day...

CHAPTER TWENTY-THREE

Marriage was supposed to be my happily-ever-after, the fairytale ending to this cautionary tale. But, like a lit match tossed into gasoline, the spark that was lit at the wedding gave way to the inferno of my addiction. It raged and consumed every waking and sleeping thought.

Somehow, I managed to hold onto my high-profile job because I was such a hard worker. However, though my job performance was exemplary, my appearance was paying the toll. In the month since the wedding, I dropped ten pounds from my already thin frame. Anytime someone expressed concern about my weight, I said I hadn't been feeling well.

I could come and go as I wanted because I was meeting my numbers, and it was part of my job to be at appointments. I left work every day exactly at 5:00 p.m. in time to get high before my family arrived home.

I always stopped off for a beer or two, which led to a bit of cocaine. Though the dosage was small, it left me edgy for the rest of the night, irritable and scared out of my mind. I didn't want to face the brutal fact I was fighting for my life again. From one moment to the next, I never knew what was going to happen or how I was going to hold it together. It was March and I was hosting an event for 88 CEOs. I tried to look as perfect as the meticulously selected decorations and arrangements, but my façade was crumbling. Spiritually weak, and physically pathetic, I clung to life. My co-workers knew I was sick and they were becoming fed up with guessing why.

I had it all figured out. A doctor medically discharged me from work as long as I sought treatment in an inpatient/outpatient program. I took a six-week absence from work and told myself I was going to go to meetings, the gym, the beach and get my game back.

But when I got to the out-patient part of treatment, I went straight back to using within three days, trying desperately to quiet the raging addiction living inside my body and mind. I no longer had any control over what I said or did. My life belonged to a power greater than me, an evil power. The Devil had me by the throat and was trying to kill me.

Yes, I only attended outpatient treatment for three days before I went on a ten-day drug spree. All hell broke loose and there was no turning back. I left home.

All I remember about that day is that I packed my suitcase and ran to my usual hideout. I packed beer, food and drugs so I wouldn't have to leave the hotel room for any reason. I was determined to get loaded and let the demon run free.

The only room they had was non-smoking which frightened me because I was sure they would smell the crack. So, I did drugs in the bathroom with the vent fan blowing.

A fellow drug addict, Judy, stopped by with more crack once I smoked everything I brought with me. While she was in my room, Chris called to check up on me. I froze, so Judy grabbed my cell phone and lied to my husband. "Mary Jane and I are going out to dinner, that's all. She will see you later."

Judy invited me over to her place where there was an abundance of drugs. The people at her house were "so unlike me," I thought. It was very rough and dangerous crowd, ex-convicts and scary people, but I didn't have anywhere else to go. In contrast to how I saw myself, these men and women had very harsh exteriors covered in tattoos, wore tattered clothing, and communicated in street language and slang that I didn't understand. They carried guns and sharp pocket knives, not afraid of being busted my police or local drug enforcement agents. I was terrified of being arrested and never wanted to meet any drug enforcement agent nose-to-nose. I wasn't privy to street politics and did not own a gun or weapon of any kind, including any kind of mace or protective spray.

Judy left her blinds open at night and that frightened me. This was a whole house of drug addicts and I thought for sure the cops would discover us. I didn't eat for ten days other than one meal from Burger King and a whole lot of popsicles. These were the only thing I could get down.

I was in touch with Chris every day, every couple of hours. Just a quick phone call from me assured him his wife was still alive. He knew the truth about what I was doing, though we didn't talk about it much. Daily, he would gently ask, "Are you ready to come home? Can you tell me where you are and I will come pick you up?"

Over those ten days, another drug buddy, Cheryl, took care of me and made sure I was safe. She drove my car and got me from one place to another. She made sure I called Chris even when I was afraid to dial his number.

The first five days are a blur but on day six, a stark fear consumed my body. Startled, I awoke around 4:00 p.m. to the sound of Oprah Winfrey's show in the background. The last time I had looked at a clock, it had been 3:30 a.m.

Oh my gosh, it's four o'clock and I lost a day, I thought. Sure enough, 12 hours had passed.

I wondered out loud if I still had a job. Then I realized I might have lost my marriage; when was the last time I'd called Chris? I knew I should phone him but I could not control my next instinct. I looked frantically under the bed for the pipe and the bag of crack cocaine stashed in the pocket of my sweatpants. Judy, my other drug buddy, was still asleep next to me.

I took a hit and insanity settled in. I was off and running again. I became paranoid with the fear that someone was peeking into the blinds of my room. My opportunity to ask for help was gone again in the rush to leave reality and my responsibilities. Reality was more than I could handle. I was in over my head and I couldn't stand the thought of facing all my wrongdoing. Judy and I had become constant companions during my last few days in hell because we were desperate for human interaction without judgment. We both knew this lifestyle was dangerous, yet neither of us was strong enough to end it.

Five or six desperately addicted people came knocking on the door with drugs of all kinds in hand. We let them in and within minutes, they were swapping stories that scared the life out of me. They were loud and foul-mouthed, and each person had been incarcerated more than once for crimes including battery, theft, drug dealing, and violence. I barely had a traffic ticket, yet my addiction to crack placed me in grave danger.

The other addicts didn't seem to have the same concerns about getting busted. They fought loudly all night and dared to take their noise outside, leaving the balcony doors open for fresh air. I just wanted to be alone, but I also feared being trapped in the silence of my own head. Judy and Cheryl stayed close to me and kept me grounded. I felt safer when one or the other was nearby. On the rare occasion, we even shared a laugh.

On day seven, I experienced a moment of clarity and realized it was Easter. I was supposed to be in Orlando at my parents' house celebrating with extended family and friends. I should have been playing with the kids having our traditional egg toss. Instead, I was ruining my husband's peace of mind.

Despite my condition, I found the strength to call Chris. He answered the phone and his voice wasn't much louder than a whisper. He was exhausted from the roller coaster of emotions. I didn't bother to lie. I told him it felt like I was dying on this Holy Day, that I was slowly fading into the void. Chris knew that yelling at me or creating any kind of confrontation would cause me to run farther away from our promise to talk every day. Chris and I had made this promise to one another during one of my early disappearing acts. He was too desperate to fight, so we both cried and promised to hold on for one more day. I felt so lonely and I got off the phone shortly after that. Talking to Chris was too painful. After hanging up, I moved into a side room and took another hit.

Chris called my parents and my brother to give them the news that once again I had fallen off the wagon. We had been married less than 90 days and I had disappeared, nowhere to be found. The battle I fought off and on for six years had come to a crossroads -- live or die.

"Mary Jane didn't know it but Chris and I started talking two or three times a day," my mom says. "I admire him. He grew up without a mom and he's a good man, a good father, a good husband, a good son-in-law. I only wished for them to hang on. I didn't want to push him to stay married to my daughter because I would never want anyone to go through what Joe and I went through."

Chris explains:

Mary Jane's dad was an insurance guy and honestly, I wanted to know what the implications were of Mary Jane having possession of my car; in legal terms, what would happen if she killed somebody while high on drugs? What would that mean for me? Could I get sued for allowing her to drive a vehicle that was now in both names? Could I lose my house and everything else because of this? I had a daughter to protect.

I quickly realized that Mary Jane's family understood my concerns. They had already been there. Chad told me to gather all her stuff and tell Mary Jane that I didn't sign up for this gig. Her family members were already at their boiling points. They pushed me to exercise tough love and to tell her that I was changing the locks on our doors.

As her new husband and soul-mate, I was crushed with fear that my new, beautiful wife would die. I would pray for hours, hoping she would make it one more day. I pleaded with God to not to take her from me and her family. I shouted to God, "You know how hard she is fighting, so bring her home to me." I would wait each day for the call and the small voice on the other end. Though I was extremely disappointed in Mary Jane, I also knew she was in the fight of her life. Mary Jane loved me; that I knew. I didn't want to give up on her because deep inside, I understood her battle was intensely bigger than what she could do alone. As her life-mate, I had to fight against the malevolent force with her, not against her.

Instead of being with my family on Easter, I spent the day with my drug dealer. She invited me to take a ride over to her grandkids' house and give them Easter baskets. *No way*, I thought. I didn't want any children seeing me looking so pathetic with unwashed hair and wrinkled clothes. I would hate to expose such innocence to the demon of addiction.

Soon after, the other addicts began talking about making a holiday meal. Even I saw how ridiculous this was. I was dining with a group of addicts who were so comfortable being high and so used to being outcast from their families that they were attempting to celebrate the day Jesus Christ was raised from the dead with booze and drugs instead of food and egg hunts.

Throughout my fellow drug addicts' distorted Easter celebration, I still recognized the importance of Easter and that I belonged to Christ. I was his child and as long as I kept fighting, the demons couldn't have me. Yet the demons were everywhere that day: near the air conditioner, behind the trees, beside the windows. These demonic entities tried to interact with me; they seemed very human. Some people would say I was just hallucinating, that I was having a psychotic break due to lack of sleep and food, fueled by my gluttonous drug use over several days, but I truly believe that demons exist in the spiritual realm. They are entities who are separated from God; they walk the spiritual streets of Hell. The only difference between us was that these spirits had actually crossed over into the afterlife and I was still physically alive. Their fates were already sealed. The Devil had deceived them.

I saw them staring at me from behind the trees. They had dark eyes and looked like real people. They appeared angry and lost, floating freely through the drug house. I could overhear them whispering my name, discussing whether or not they should harm me. I saw a woman with long brown hair, hunched over, wearing a free-flowing garment. She was standing in one place and I couldn't get her to look at me no matter what I said.

I saw a tall, thin young man dressed in black clothes, leaning against a truck. He had a smirk on his face as he stared in my direction. His arms were folded and he appeared to be waiting for me to become more vulnerable, mentally and spiritually. He wanted me to lose my mind as the night grew darker. I knew he was doomed to live in Hell and had nowhere to go, but as there is no reference to time in Hell, so he stood there patiently and watched my every move. Job 4:14-17 says, "Fear came upon me, and trembling, which made all my bones shake. Then a spirit passed before my face; the hair on my body stood up. It stood still, But, I could not discern its appearance. A form *was* before my eyes: *There was* silence; then a voice *saying*: 'Can a mortal be more righteous than God? Can a man be more pure than his Maker?'"

At 4:00 a.m., outside along the lonely stairwell, I finally spoke to the entity out loud. "I am still a child of God, even though I struggle," I shouted. "You cannot take me to the dark side. I will not give up my faith in Christ, even now. The Lord will rescue me from my darkness and my addiction, and I will be redeemed."

I knew this was a spiritual battle. I knew the truth, and wasn't about to let go of my rights as a child of God. Over the past nine days, I had been on my knees more than once praying for deliverance. I did not want to die in active addiction. I didn't want someone I loved to find me dead in a chair or on the floor. A part of me wanted to go home and see my husband and my stepdaughter, but I couldn't get myself to leave. I was a prisoner who no longer spoke normally due to the drugs in my system, and the lack of sleep and food. But I knew that it couldn't go on forever. Sooner or later someone would come find me, whether it was the police, my family or Satan himself.

Exhausted, I packed up my drugs, left the drug house and checked into a hotel; yet, in my suite, I detected an intense smell of masculine cologne. Every hair on my body stood up and I was aware there was a malevolent spirit in the room. "In the name of Jesus," I proclaimed, "This is not going to end this way. Get out of my room and my life." The strong aroma of cologne lingered, and I second-guessed myself into thinking a man was actually in my room. I looked under the bed, behind the couch, in the shower and in the closets. No human being hid in the room. Yet, the stomach-churning scent remained. I can still remember the smell; it was a cheap musky male fragrance. I realized it was a demonic spirit. In that moment, I thought of my fourteenth birthday. The demons I had unleashed by using the Ouija board had finally found me and were coming to collect their debt— my soul.

I heard two male voices conversing back and forth. "Do you think we can take her now? Do you think she's ready?" they asked each other.

"No, I'm not!" I yelled back. Some may say it was "only" the drugs talking. However, the Bible speaks clearly of these demons and unclean spirits. There are many books confirming that vicious spirits are trapped on this Earthly realm. Because of my disobedience over the years, wavering back and forth in faith, playing with dangerous drugs, and surrounding myself with atheist and agnostic mentalities, my life reflected a woman who had once believed but found herself on dangerous ground. My spiritual battle aligned with the person described in the book of Matthew 12: 43-45, "When an unclean spirit goes out of a man, he goes through dry places, seeking rest and finds none. Then he says, 'I will return to my house from which I came.' And when he comes, he finds it empty, swept, and put in order. Then he goes and takes with him seven others spirits more wicked than himself, and they enter and dwell there; and the last state of that man is worse than the first. So shall it be with this wicked generation." My state of being was grave. My battle was more intense now, as my house, *my body and mind*, was no longer in order. So I prayed for help, reciting a memorized prayer over and over as a mantra.

On day nine, my car was stolen, apparently by another addict or dealer. I was so afraid of telling Chris I called everyone I knew from my world of sinful addiction. Of course, they all denied knowing anything about the car's disappearance.

I walked to the front desk of the hotel lobby and asked them to call the police. I had a hard time filling out the paperwork because I couldn't focus. The female cop didn't seem surprised that my car was gone; in fact, she appeared rather suspicious. I was petrified she would ask the hotel management for my room number and begin a search of my room. This was not her first time dealing with an addict's missing car.

The person who helped me through filing the police report was Cheryl. She was the closest thing to a real "friend" I had in the drug world. She knew my insecurities and fears, and helped settle my nerves and my insanity for moments at a time. She reminded me when it was time to call my husband, though I never told him exactly where I was because I felt like I was protecting both of us.

Consumed by the fierce energy active addiction requires, I wished everyone who cared about me would just leave me alone and abandon me altogether so I could finally stop feeling guilty. I was so tired of fighting. I just wanted this whole, cruel life to be over.

CHAPTER TWENTY-FOUR

My car hadn't been stolen. Turns out Chris came and "repossessed" it, following the advice of my parents and friends, Kerrie and George, who had years' more experience dealing with a chaotic drug addict bent on self-destruction.

George told the wide-eyed Chris that if he took away my wheels, the charade would eventually end. "Her fellow druggies are 'running buddies.' As soon as her car is gone, they'll run," he said. "Her vehicle is like currency: it's the one thing of value she possesses."

Chris explains his side:

I knew of all the hotels and motels in the area, and I called every one of them asking to speak with to my wife through her maiden name. If that didn't work, I called back and asked for her under our married name. That did the trick for a while until Mary Jane caught on to my M.O.

I got desperate and asked George to ride with me and help me search for her car. We drove to every place in town and finally found the vehicle parked outside a hotel. We drove off to George's place and hid it.

I felt tired and very abandoned during this time. Though I knew Mary Jane was extremely sick, I was exhausted from lack of sleep. I was jaded and disillusioned, wondering if she would ever get well. I resented seeing my wife running in and out of this hotel with criminals and drug addicts who didn't care if she lost her job, or got arrested, or ultimately lost her life. George convinced me that breaking into the hotel room would only create chaos, and neither George nor I wanted to go to jail from beating up one of these scumbags. I had to trust the process that with no car, Mary Jane would call me for help.

A few hours later, Mary Jane called. She asked if I had taken the car and I said "no." She said she was calling the cops. I told her to go ahead and do that — did she, and her friends, want the police showing up, asking questions?

That's when she knew the gig was up. I told her I didn't want her at the house and at the advice of her parents, I was changing all the locks on the doors. And that's just what I did later on that day.

My drug run ended where the first chapter of this book began, hallucinating and half out of my mind in that demolished hotel room. After a night of seeing demons in the trees and inside the air conditioning unit, yanking pictures off the walls, throwing the mattresses off the beds, I was finally done. I had run out of drugs and was ready to surrender. I found the courage to call Chris and told him it was over.

Climbing in his truck, Chris delivered an ultimatum: "You can either go back upstairs and continue your journey towards hell, or come with me to treatment." I didn't have the energy to refuse his conditions. Defeated and exhausted, I surrendered to Chris's plan. Though my body throbbed with pain from the drugs, my heart stopped hurting. I knew I was on my journey home.

Armed with a suitcase, Chris hastily packed clothes that belonged to his preteen daughter. That's how small and sickly I became; a 30-year-old woman shriveled to the same size as an 11-year-old girl.

Though I accepted Chris's ultimatum without resistance, I became really nasty with "this Susan woman" from the treatment center. She told me I needed to come in immediately. "Just give me a day to sleep and I will consider it," I bargained, suddenly concerned Chris would leave me upon my entrance to treatment. My emotions and mind were totally maxed out and I became irrational. I screamed – literally – into the phone and demanded rest and food. Chris told me he would take me to another hotel but not back to the house. We checked into a hotel and I showered. Of course, Chris refused to leave. He watched me sleep from 2:00 p.m. through the next morning, for 13 hours straight.

He got me up and dressed me for treatment. I begged for more sleep, but he wasn't having it. He was finished with this nonsense. The offer was the same. I could go to treatment or go back to the hell I had been living.

The pain I felt getting out of the shower the day before was only the beginning of the tenderness I felt as my feet hit the ground after sleeping all those hours. My legs and feet were so sore I could hardly walk. Brushing my hair actually hurt. My gums were tender as the toothbrush swept across each tooth.

Chris asked to examine my body to see if I had been beaten. I refused to let him see me naked because I was so ashamed of what I looked like. I rushed to the shower, locked the door, and undressed there. As the water poured over my battered body, the reality of what I had done overwhelmed me. I was no longer welcome in my own home. I was a safety issue to my own stepdaughter. I had exceeded my husband's trust and his boundaries – no more ten-day runs, no more lies, no more drugs, no more hotel rescues. It was over.

I could hardly stand in the shower because my legs were so weak, and my feet and ankles hurt. My hip bones protruded from lack of food, and my chin and face were sore to the touch. My teeth and ears hurt. My fingertips were cut and burnt. Overwhelmed with fatigue,

I stepped out of the water, dried off and took a look at myself in the large mirror. All I saw was a tattered woman with tired eyes, drawn cheeks and scabs on my chin. My body was just about dead. That my heart didn't give out is a true miracle. I had given my body every reason to stop functioning properly and I had done my nervous system serious harm with the drugs, alcohol and lack of sleep.

Just three months prior, I wore a bridal gown and stood next to my knight-in-shining-armor. The candlelit service was a dreamy memory at this point. Today there was no soft music sung by friends, scripture being read, no minister talking about happily-ever-after. These were dim memories from what felt like decades ago.

Why Chris didn't leave me alone to die was beyond me. I guess the commitment he had made before God and the church only 75 days earlier kept him in the marriage. I would have understood if he checked out. I could only imagine when he agreed to stay with me "for better or for worse" that he never imagined how heartbreaking "worse" was.

In the mirror I asked myself, "Do I go into treatment, or take my chances and go it on my own?" My mind traveled in and out of my options. One moment, I considered the promise of getting better and restoring peace to my life. The next moment, I was frantic with thoughts of "What have I done?" "How did I get here?" and "What does my future have in store?" I could hardly breathe as I weighed my choices.

I was full of both gratitude and anger when I decided Watershed Treatment Center was my destination. I would live in a hospital setting, not for a couple days but what may be months. I had been down this long, winding road where therapists demand details and truth, freedom disappears, men withdraw, family members recoil, and employers fire people – like me.

My family was so relieved Chris took the hard-line approach with me. My dad:

Leigh had more conversations with Chris than I did. I think if she had not told Chris everything we had been through with Mary Jane, he may have responded differently. I don't know what the outcome would have been. His response was exactly what it should have been. He took a stand and said, "You're not coming home!" I praise him and respect him for that. I'm sure that was a tough decision, but it was the right thing to do.

Kerrie:

I knew Chris was at his limit and I knew Mary Jane didn't want to lose him or the marriage. Despite her behavior in addiction, she loved Chris very much. Chris was adamant with her and she knew he meant business. It scared Mary Jane, and that fear was a good thing for her.

Chris and I went to visit Mary Jane in rehab and celebrated his birthday sitting out on a little patio. She said she hated for me to see her there. It was humbling for her. But I love her, no matter what. It was the first time I thought that maybe this was going to work. I definitely knew this was where she needed to be.

The love and support from my family and friends held me up during my time in rehab. But it was a conversation I had two weeks after checking in that changed my life forever.

"Sit down in that chair," Dr. Getty said. I took a seat in the cafeteria. "Mary Jane, I'm going to share something with you and you have to listen. I've been doing this for twenty years. Never in my life have I met someone who is as heartbroken and distraught as your husband Chris. I'm here to tell you that Chris is not a man that is going to watch you go in and out of treatment for a lifetime. He's going to have to say goodbye to you, because he physically doesn't have it in him to watch you come and go in hospitals. He's completely heartbroken and he's wondering what the fuck he's gotten himself into. As a man, I can tell you what he's thinking. But he loves you more than life and if you want recovery, his commitment to you and your marriage is solid.

"Your life is like a crystal ball. Inside that ball, there's a person who has had a more amazing life than anyone I've ever met in my work. You have shared some incredible life moments and shared great success in your time. But the ball is completely cracked with hairline fractures and if you ever relapse again, it'll be the ping that shatters it completely.

"Your life will never look or sound the same again. You will lose Chris, Olivia, your family, your career, your freedom and possibly your life. I need you to go back to your room, get on your knees, and ask yourself what life means to you. Do you want Chris in your life? Do you want your job? Do you want Olivia as a daughter? Do you want live your life coming in and out of hospitals and treatment centers? If anyone of these areas is important to you, you must know the truth about what I see."

My heart plunged into my stomach as I went back to my room. I got on my knees and it was there, for the first time, I knew I had what it takes to get clean. I felt the gentle nudging of the Holy Spirit, also known as *The Spirit of Truth,* and a refreshed sense of hope. Kneeling alongside my bed, I intently prayed for a new life. The remorse and reality of what I had done and who I had become set in. I sat for a long time in that silent room with Dr. Getty's words echoing through my head.

After intense soul-searching, I fell into a deep depression as I fretted about the repercussions of my actions towards Chris. Motivated by this concern, I completed all the assigned work and asked for additional ways I could create change. I finally faced my personal Four Horsemen: Terror, Bewilderment, Frustration, and Despair. Facing each horseman head on, I became willing to reveal the intense pain

I still carried from my past. I admitted that like a prisoner sentenced to life behind bars, I too had given up my dreams long ago. I cried healing tears on many days.

As I cried, I remembered a line from Dickens's *Great Expectations*: "Heaven knows we need never be ashamed of our tears, for they are rain upon the blinding dust of earth, overlying our hard hearts." My grief was satisfied and carried away by my tears. I stood before judge and jury, willing to own up to my sins, and accept the consequences.

My counselors were amazed by my zeal. Any free moment I had between attending 12-Step meetings and completing assignments, I spent in prayer and reflection. I knew that my work towards rebuilding my character was a daily process and felt my relationship with Christ was reborn. I never thought I'd feel optimistic again, but every day I stayed sober, this little mustard seed of hope grew and flourished in my soul.

But this growth was not my work alone. Besides the counselors and other addiction behavior technicians, Chris dedicated hours to seeing me, attending joint therapy sessions and just loving me back to sanity. He was my biggest supporter and fan as I crossed sobriety's mile markers.

The transition back towards a healthy, trusting marriage did not come overnight. As I did the footwork required to live abundantly, we worked on communication and recreating normal daily living. I had a lot to prove to him and to those around me. He and I took a team approach to sobriety since we knew it affected the whole family. We talked openly about our concerns, challenges and the fledgling hope for an incredible life.

I really believe my marriage helped break the curse I had been living under for ten years. Scripture talks about how the braid of three is harder to sever than a strand of one or two. Ecclesiastes 4:12 states, "A person standing alone can be attacked and defeated, but two can stand back-to-back and conquer." Three are even better, for a triple-braided cord is not easily broken." When Chris and I took our vows, the darkness in me no longer had just *me* to deal with. It was Chris and me. It was that vow we took before Christ, and the deep bond it forged, that actually saved me. The darkness that had followed me for years had been banished. When I walked out of treatment after four weeks, I was released from the bondage of self-destruction, of my demons, of my addiction. The Four Dark Horsemen who once determined my conduct now stood behind Four Devout Warriors: Honesty, Integrity, Gratitude, and Hope. Through the Spirit of Truth, I humbly grew in relationship with God -- and I was finally free.

EPILOGUE

My spiritual journey and my transformation made all of the pain worthwhile, because now I can share it openly with others who also suffer from addiction or other challenges. There is no shame anymore when I talk about how I behaved inside my sinful life; I believe in my soul that the other side of this coin is a grateful and honorable life. I am forever thankful to my parents, brother, husband, daughter and friends who stuck by my side, and I am committed to living my remaining time on earth *showing* my thankfulness through sharing with every human being that our God is a God of second chances, a God of love, and a God of transformations. *Our God is one of transformations.*

In Corinthians, 3:18 the Bible says, "But we all, with unveiled face, beholding as in a mirror the glory of the Lord, are being transformed into the same image from glory to glory, just as by the Spirit of the Lord."

In my old life, I used to live in fear that all men could see my sin, terrified that if people knew my sinful past, their judgment would be harsh and damning. Because of that fear, I lived within self-protective walls that hindered my spiritual growth and silenced my truth. I refused to believe that someone with such an ugly past could live abundantly and with unlimited potential in God.

Today, I live without walls of omission and deceit. The only reason I am masking my true identity is out of respect for my family, husband, and daughter. I live in complete freedom because I surrendered by admitting my life wasn't working, and God broke the bonds of failure upon my life. I can walk freely among my peers with God holding my head up high and my back straight. I have been brought safely back home.

My definition of transformation and coming home to God may be different from yours, because I see it as a changed state of mind. I am the embodiment of 2 Corinthians 5:17. "All things have passed away, and behold all things have become new." As a new creation in Christ, I have the freedom to walk more generously from the systems of thought that seek to control and confuse us through false teachings and philosophies.

Friends, there is a big difference between living with redemption and living *in* freedom. By definition, redemption means "to regain possession of" or "to atone." My faith taught me Christ has paid the penalty for the transgressions of man by dying on the cross, and that all I need do to receive redemption was to believe in Him. By definition, freedom means, "liberation from slavery or restraint" or "from the power of another."

Though I was raised in a Christ-centered, faith-based household, I lived like a woman who never knew Christ or God ever existed, worshipping the golden calf of drugs, money, career titles and popularity to fill my empty soul. But I was always redeemed; if my addiction or any other accident had killed me, I would have met my Creator in Heaven.

However, I didn't live in the freedom that God originally intended. I lived bound to my own desires and hindrances. I lived a life of containment and mistaken identity. I lived a life where others influenced my habits and activities to the point of destruction and self-sabotage. I lived a life other people wanted for me. I lived a life under systems of thought based on lies and deceit. The truth was never "in" me in a way that I could defend my mind, will and emotions from those influences; I failed to know the Word and the Spirit of God. I wanted spirituality, success and sobriety handed to me on a silver platter instead of working for them myself. I did not know the two Commandments in the New Testament Bible or practice the 12 Steps and 12 Principles of a recovery program. I learned the hard way that we cannot deliver ourselves from sin or mistaken identity and we cannot have an anointed freedom unless we, too, know God personally and intimately.

As illustrated in these past chapters, I tried every way possible to "fix" myself, whether it was a better job, better relationship, more friends, more social events, a better wardrobe, a better apartment, etc. But these were merely temporary solutions -- never substantial or long-lasting. I still had that nagging hole in my heart. I was a slave to quick fixes.

What are you a slave to today? Common problems like gluttony, poor discipline over finances, deprived health habits and poor communication in our families and businesses are killing our dreams of abundant living. Offenses such as pornography, theft, drugs, white-collar crimes and driving under the influence are stealing our good standing in the communities which we serve. We are caving to thought processes and behaviors that keep us from God's best in our lives because we lack the truth. John 12:31 tells us that Satan is the "ruler of this world." Satan is the major influence on the mind-set expressed by the ideals, opinions, goals and views of many people who are apart from God. His areas of influence also encompass the world's philosophies, education and commerce. The thoughts and false religions of the world are under his control and have sprung from his lies and deceptions.

If you've learned anything from my story, I hope it is that the way to freedom is transformation, through a renewal of our minds and a relationship with God. The Bible promises, in Romans, Chapter 12:2 "And do not be conformed to this world, but be transformed by the renewing of your mind, that you may prove what is the good and acceptable and perfect will of God." This renewal is one that will complete the transformation. This promise changed my inward dialogue and my outward life forever; I no longer have the urges that demand to be acted out.

Friend, what are you holding onto today that keeps you from God's very best in your life? What distracts you today and keeps you away from spending time in the church, synagogue or place of worship?

One of my distractions was pride. For a long time, I told others (and myself) that I had it all together. The pride was so deeply ingrained, I couldn't see it. A woman name Riesa, who served as an addiction therapist, once told me to go home from a session because I walked in "dressed to the nines." She yelled, "You don't look like a woman who is dying! Go home and come back when you can be honest." I had no idea what she meant until years later. I finally recognized that the outward manifestation of my pride was my false exterior: a superficial, counterfeit smile with an expensive designer outfit. I was trying to hide my inner struggle with low self-esteem, high self-concern, drugs and alcohol by dressing up in expensive clothes and driving fancy cars. I honestly did not realize how closely I was walking to spiritual and physical death.

My spirit was weak because the power of God in my life was so limited, due to distractions, false doctrine and chemical addiction. The only thing I cared about was saving my public reputation. I wasn't interested in changing because that was too hard. So I remained a slave to my own thoughts and their destructive outcomes. In the process of trying to save my outer reputation, suffering an addict's death seemed my fate most days.

Dear reader, God wants all His children today, and in the ages to come, to have a way of complete *redemption and freedom*. God is a gentleman and honors His word, allowing us to choose how we will relate to Him, and if we will believe in Him – at all. We must choose. Do we live our life at an arm's length from God, never truly understanding Him, His word and His intentions for us? I ask you, are you abiding by God's Divine Mission for you?

When I was 14 and God literally gave me direction that I would write a book, I had absolutely no idea it would be a book based on my failures.

I would have never believed, as a teenager, I would encounter so much pain and turmoil yet happily live to tell about it. Not only did God command me to share my story of victory in a small room with those who can relate to my trials, but to the world. This never interested me in any way. It took me ten years to obey the call of God because I was petrified of what you thought of me. I was self-absorbed about how this story would affect me publicly, so it rarely occurred to me I was supposed to share this story to glorify *God's work in me*. It is God who gets the credit, not me. God pursued me in my journey through hell to bring hope so that I could come back home and live abundantly *now*.

My story is about one life that has a purpose; just like your life has an intention. Like me, you probably have big dreams about what you want your end-life to look like.

I encourage you to believe that God wants your success and your dreams. No matter what you think you have done or where you think you have been, God is calling you "home." God desires that you live in freedom from the temptation that haunts you in this world, be it drugs, like my sin, or any other character defect that keeps you out of the sunlight of the Spirit. I fully believe that a relationship with God and His word can change any worldly habit.

John 8 tells us that "If you remain in my word, you will truly be my disciples, and you will know the truth, and the truth will make you free."

The original word *make* means "a work in progress." Through the renewing of my mind, I began to think and act differently in my daily life. God delivered me instantaneously, but I had to learn how to behave like a woman who was sober, and theologically sound. The moment I asked God for help, my request was immediately granted. I didn't suddenly walk in freedom because I lacked knowledge of God's promises. However, over time, I matured in my walk with God through prayer, education, going to 12-Step meetings, studying books on spiritual growth and reading the Bible. I was *"made"* more free. The more truth that is "in" me, the freer I become. The same it is with you, my friend. The more time you spend in relationship with God, the freer you will be to fulfill God's purpose for your life.

God is as alive today as He was in the Old Testament, and there are miracles taking place for those who believe miracles *can* happen. We are fortunate enough to be living out the blessings of the New Testament.

For example, surviving my drug addiction is a miracle. Writing this book without shame is a miracle. My intention for this book is to let someone know that we all sin and fall short of God's best. We all have the shadows that we would prefer no one see. However, be encouraged. No matter what you have done in your own journey through life, you, too, can come to God and be transformed. You can experience the redemption and the freedom God always intended. We serve a God of second chances.

I spoke of coming home to God throughout this story. Similar to the story of the prodigal son, to come home and receive transformation simply means admitting life with God is incredibly better than a life alone. To come home and be transformed means to begin fulfilling your purpose by asking the question, "What does my Creator want for my life?" instead of asking, "What do I want for my life?" To have a transformation is to return to the basic text of the Word of God, and begin a relationship with our Creator. Then we become informed as to how men can live, and what we are truly capable of under the influence of the Spirit of Deity. Only then, can we begin to understand God's full intention for mankind from the beginning of time. For me, being transformed and coming home meant to be in right standing with my family and the world. Transformation is a state of mind, knowing that I am not creating division among my parents, my friends, or my family. Transformation is being comfortable in my own skin, believing that I have a divine purpose. My life's transformation is living among people and allowing each person the independence to experience their own journey without condemning their choices. Experiencing transformation is a life-long passage.

Walking through spiritual hell is a long journey where those who are lost in spirit look aimlessly for a distraction in a person, chemical substances, food, material items or a career to fill their soul. Their minds, their will and their emotions are clouded with deception, believing they can live with their own set of truths and still have a life of freedom. Walking through Hell, apart from God, is to waiver back and forth without ever truly feeling fulfilled, loved and understood. Being separated from our Creator is to spend years trying to accomplish a dream that never comes true because of a self-sabotaging behavior.

Scripture warns us in John 10:10 "The thief does not come except to steal, and to kill, and to destroy." The power of Satan almost killed me. I am sure of it. I lived in order to tell the next victim of Satan's lies, and that life in the Word of God is profoundly more sufficient than a life without it. Satan comes in the form of many appealing distractions; he offers counterfeit promises he cannot fulfill, (Genesis 3: 4-5), he rules the masses outside of God's protection (Ephesians 2:1-3), he seeks an opportune time to tempt us (Luke 4:13), and he tries to hide the actual truth about our God (2 Corinthians 4:3-4). He knows he will lose the final battle against God. So, his focus now is to distract and deceive as many people until the final battle of Armageddon where, according to the book of Revelation chapter 20:10, "And the Devil who deceived them was cast into the lake of fire and brimstone, where the beast and the false prophet *are,* and shall be tormented day and night forever and ever."

I know I am not perfect. I don't live with my head in the clouds, convinced I am an untouchable human being. I feelings still get hurt, I still get discouraged, I still become weary, and I have many life lessons that lie ahead. Yet, because of my God, I live with a new sense of hope and joy despite the tough days. My life, and the way I walk through it, transformed because of God and His word.

The book of Philippians, chapter 3, verse 12-16, defines my new life wonderfully.

"It is not that I have already taken hold of it or have already attained perfect maturity, but I continue my pursuit in hope that I may possess it, since I have indeed been taken possession of by Christ. Brothers, I for my part do not consider myself to have taken pursuit toward the possession. Just one thing: forgetting what lies behind but straining forward to what lies ahead, I continue my pursuit toward the goal, the prize of Gods upward calling, in Christ Jesus."

Friends, God loves you as much as He loves me. A life of complete redemption and freedom awaits you. This book, *Transformed*, was inspired by God, for God's Glory.

My story of willfulness apart from God proves that He loved me despite my behaviors. God pursued me into the gates of hell. He walked alongside me, while showing me love, forgiveness and grace.

My friends, be encouraged. If you wandered off the anointed path, ask God for help. Your own transformation begins with the simple words: "God, please help me." I am *living proof* of the power of that prayer.

Whoever you are, wherever you are, may you be blessed on your journey and may that journey always bring you home.

Amen.